The

Terry Johnson is a playwright and director. His dozen major theatre awards include a Tony for Best Director for *La Cage Aux Folles*, and Oliviers for Best Comedy for *Hysteria* and *Cleo, Camping, Emmanuelle and Dick*. He is a former Literary Associate at the Royal Court where five of his own plays – *Insignificance*, *Cries from the Mammal House*, *Hysteria*, *Hitchcock Blonde* and *Piano/Forte* – were first staged. *Imagine Drowning*, *Dead Funny*, *Prism*, *Ken* and a version of *Uncle Vanya* all premiered at Hampstead, and *Cleo, Camping, Emmanuelle and Dick* and his adaptation of *The London Cuckolds* at the National Theatre. West End credits include *Mrs Henderson Presents*, *The Duck House*, *End of the Rainbow*, *The Prisoner of Second Avenue*, *The Rise and Fall of Little Voice*, *Rain Man*, *Whipping It Up*, *One Flew Over the Cuckoo's Nest*, *Hitchcock Blonde*, *The Graduate*, *Dead Funny*, *Hysteria*, *Elton John's Glasses* and *The Memory of Water*. In 2014 he celebrated the fiftieth anniversary of Joan Littlewood's Theatre Workshop with revivals at Stratford East of *Oh What a Lovely War* and *Fings Ain't Wot They Used T'Be*.

by the same author
from Faber

UNCLE VANYA
(after Chekhov)

TERRY JOHNSON

The Sex Party

faber

First published in 2022
by Faber and Faber Limited
74–77 Great Russell Street
London WC1B 3DA

Typeset by Brighton Gray
Printed and bound in the UK by CPI Group (Ltd), Croydon CR0 4YY

A CIP record for this book
is available from the British Library

978-0-571-38268-2

The Sex Party was first performed at the Menier Chocolate Factory, London, on 4 November 2022, with the following cast:

Gilly Lisa Dwan
Alex Jason Merrells
Jake John Hopkins
Hetty Molly Osborne
Jeff Timothy Hutton
Magdalena Amanda Donohoe
Tim Will Barton
Camilla Kelly Price
Lucy Pooya Mohseni

Director Terry Johnson
Set and Costume Designer Tim Shortall
Lighting Designer Ben Ormerod
Sound Designer John Leonard
Associate Director Georgie Rankcom

Characters

Alex
late forties, comfortably off, academic

Hetty
early thirties, bubbly, ex-dancer, photographer

Gilly
mid-forties, handsome, housewife

Jake
late forties, casual conservative, teacher

Jeff
mid-fifties, strong-jawed American, business consultant

Magdalena
mid-forties, Russian, wiry, attractive, wife

Tim
early forties, amiable, actor and phone sales

Camilla
late forties, austere, painter, arts and craft supplies

Lucy
mid-forties, angular, quiet, dignified

Setting

The kitchen.

There are bottles and glasses in formation, and a covered buffet. During the action the drinks become increasingly disarrayed and the buffet gets uncovered and demolished.

THE SEX PARTY

Note

When dialogue lines are unspaced,
the characters are speaking simultaneously.

Throughout the play, levels of inebriation vary but steadily
increase, and people look at their mobile phones a lot.

Act One

8.00 p.m.
  Alex and Hetty.
  Gilly and Jake.

Gilly We're VERY nervous.

Alex Don't be. Jake!

Jake Hi.

Alex Nice to meet you.

Gilly Shitting a brick.

Alex This is Hetty.

Hetty Hi.

Gilly Hi. Hello.

Jake Hello. Jake.

Hetty Hello.

Alex Did you say shitting a brick?

Gilly Yes. A bit.

Hetty So did I. The first time.

Gilly You shit a brick?

Hetty Well, not literally.

Alex *and* **Gilly** Obviously.

Hetty But, you know.

Alex Red, white, fizz, beer?

Gilly Fizz!

3

Jake A beer, if you've got one.

Alex It's a prosecco.

Gilly Prosecco is fine.

Alex Hetty prefers a prosecco.

Gilly Anything. Honestly. Fill a glass.

Alex The thing to remember . . .

Gilly This *is* our first time.

Alex . . . is the thing I messaged you.

Gilly Which thing?

Jake I've not been privy to any of these messages.

Gilly Yes you have; I showed you them.

Alex The thing is: you surrender nothing at the door.

Gilly That's what I told him.

Alex Everything's consensual. Obviously.

Gilly Obviously.

Hetty That's a given.

Gilly Or someone would go to jail, presumably.

Alex In this day and age, probably.

Hetty Probably.

Pause.

Jake Well, in any day and age, one would hope.

Gilly Hopefully. Anyway. Don't expect me to bail you out.

Alex If you want to sit in the corner and drink wine, you can both just sit in the corner and drink wine.

Jake Well, we might do a bit more than that, obviously.

Gilly Obviously. Or we wouldn't be here.

Jake Obviously.

Gilly But I will need a drink. Or three.

Jake We got here, anyway.

Alex And you're here as a couple.

Jake Yes.

Alex And that's fine.

Jake The two of us.

Gilly Same old, same old.

Jake Afraid so.

Alex Drinks.

Jake Cheers.

Gilly You're driving.

Jake I know.

Gilly I'm drinking; so you're definitely driving because I'm *definitely* drinking.

Hetty Chin-chin.

Gilly And what do you do, um . . .?

Hetty Hetty.

Gilly Sorry.

Hetty I'm Hetty, and I'm a photographer.

Gilly Well; I'm Gilly and I'm an alcoholic.

Jake She is, in fact.

Gilly No, I'm not.

Alex Hetty does food porn.

Gilly Food porn?

Hetty Not what it sounds like.

Jake Porn? With food?

Alex No, no. She gets a commission for . . . Frosties . . .

Hetty Well, not Frosties . . . not Nestlé.

Jake Conscience.

Hetty Out of my league.

Alex But some generic cereal . . .

Hetty Tesco's Own . . .

Alex Tesco's Own Sugary Whatevers . . . she goes to Tesco's, buys the Frosties . . .

Hetty The Whatevers.

Alex Puts them in a bowl, pours the milk on, couple of raspberries . . .

Hetty Three.

Alex Three raspberries . . .

Hetty Or seven. Never even, always odd.

Gilly Sounds fascinating.

Alex She can make anything look delicious.

Hetty Except curry.

Alex Apparently.

Hetty The better you light a dhansak, the more it looks like sick.

Jake Lovely.

Hetty Unless you take the chicken out, rinse it under the tap and put it back on top. But even then.

Jake So; who's coming?

Alex Yes, that's . . .

Gilly Who else *is* coming? I may not look it but I'm *very* nervous.

Alex You don't look it.

Gilly I've made a very good effort, I think.

Hetty You look fabulous.

Gilly Don't you think?

Alex You look terrific.

Jake You look fine.

Gilly Don't get too effusive.

Jake I meant it.

Hetty She looks wonderful.

Jake That's what I said.

Gilly Well it wasn't, but I do, but I'm very nervous.

Alex You say that, but why don't I believe you?

Pause.

Jake And who else?

Alex Well, there's Eliana and Svet. Very experienced.

Gilly That's a good thing, is it?

Alex He's Yugoslavian originally, she's Italian. They've got a coffee shop.

Hetty I don't know them either.

Alex Free trade, top notch. They're nice. You'll like them.

Gilly Do they know we're not . . . you know . . .

Alex Swapping?

Hetty Don't say swapping!

Gilly Swapping.

Hetty Don't say that word!

Alex They do. And I'll remind them.

Gilly We're not swappers.

Jake We're not swingers.

Gilly Don't say that word either.

Hetty I *know*.

Gilly We're neither, we're just . . .

Jake Curious.

Gilly No! That's one of those words too, isn't it?

Jake It's *a* word, yes.

Alex It *is* a word, yes.

Gilly One of the words you use.

Alex Well, that's what you technically are.

Jake Curious, then.

Gilly No! We're just . . . curious. With a little c. Not as in Curious, you know; with a big C.

Jake Anyone else?

Alex Magdalena and Jeff. She's Russian. He's American.

Jake Russian? Is she?

Gilly Let's not get *too* curious.

Jake Whose idea *was* this?

Gilly What are they like?

Alex I haven't met them.

Gilly Have you met them?

Hetty I haven't met any of these people.

Gilly So then how do you meet these people?

Hetty He hasn't met them.

Gilly You haven't met them?

Alex Well, not all of them.

Jake You mean anyone might rock up?

Alex Not anyone. We're on a website.

Gilly And?

Hetty You wink at people. And they wink back, or they don't. They tend not to wink back at Alex but they all wink back at me.

Alex You post an event, they ask for an invite, you ignore them, or invite them.

Gilly But you've never met them?

Hetty People are usually nice.

Gilly Well, they'd need to be.

Hetty Yes; they would.

Gilly Wouldn't they?

Alex They will be.

Hetty You get the odd one.

Jake One what?

Gilly Odd how?

Jake How odd?

Hetty Oh, you know. One to avoid. It's like anywhere.

Alex People usually turn out to be good people.

Gilly Yes, but they don't any more, do they? People are a lot less nice lately.

Hetty I know.

Gilly Suddenly everyone knows everything about things they know nothing about.

Alex That'll be that pesky internet I've heard tell of.

Gilly Public forum? It's a bloody cage fight.

Alex The only problem with democracy . . .

Gilly Are the fuckwits. My erudition is not trumped by your ignorance.

Jake That's certainly how it is in our house.

Alex Our entire culture, dictated by Twitter.

Gilly And you can't even wrap tomorrow's chips in it. If all these mad opinions are indulged, freedom of speech is done for.

Alex I don't think you've thought that through.

Gilly I don't have to. It's blindingly obvious.

Alex I don't know what I ever saw in you.

Jake If you see it again, give us a clue.

Gilly Ha. Ha.

Hetty Do we have to be serious? I don't want to be serious.

Jake Me neither. We'll be not serious together. Anyone else turning up?

Alex There's a young couple I know; Jake and Rebecca.

Gilly Another Jake!

Hetty Two Jakes.

Jake Don't get us mixed up.

Gilly I'll try not to.

Jake They gave you the wink, did they?

Alex I know Jake from work.

Jake And you what, you just *asked* him?

Alex In the pub.

Gilly Does *she* know what she's in for?

Hetty Apparently.

Alex Then there's Tim. And Camilla. I know Tim. I don't know Camilla. And then a few maybes.

Gilly Well, we're not spoilt for choice, are we?

Jake Not that we intend to do any choosing, darling – do we, darling?

Gilly We already chose – didn't we, sweetie?

Jake Yes we did.

Gilly No more choosing.

Hetty I'm not choosy.

Alex I've noticed.

Hetty Well, I am . . .

Alex She is.

Hetty In fact, I'm *very* choosy. It's just every so often I choose *not* to be.

Alex Oh, and there's Lucy. A woman I met.

Hetty Random.

Alex In Coco de Mer.

Hetty Oh well then. Everyone loves a unicorn.

Jake More the merrier, then.

Gilly I love what you're wearing.

Hetty Thank you.

Gilly I didn't really know what to wear.

Hetty You look fabulous.

Gilly Never got dressed to get undressed before. I've been in the wardrobe since mid-afternoon.

Hetty In the wardrobe?

Gilly Walk-in wardrobe.

Hetty Oh, you lucky thing.

Jake Otherwise known as upstairs.

Gilly Anyway; I finally made up my mind.

Jake That's a slight exaggeration. We got as far as the front door.

Gilly I panicked. You were no bloody use. I've got another two outfits in my bag.

Hetty Ooh. Can I see?

Alex Fashion show!

Hetty You'll be lucky.

Alex Only if you fancy it.

Hetty Don't put your bossy boots on.

Alex I thought you liked me in them.

Gilly Right. Is there a place where I can . . .?

Jake You look fine as you are.

Alex You look fabulous.

Hetty Let me show you the living room. We've gone to town a bit. Fairy grotto in the garden.

Alex You and your fairy grotto.

Hetty If it gets too loud we'll close the French windows.

Gilly Loud?

Hetty Follow me!

Gilly I'm so bloody nervous.

Hetty I know.

Gilly Comes over me in waves.

  Exit Gilly and Hetty.

Alex Need another?

Jake Driving.

Alex Ah.

Jake Thanks for the invite.

Alex My pleasure.

Jake I mean, we never would have.

Alex I know.

Jake If you hadn't.

Alex Which is why I asked.

Jake Hats off for asking.

Alex There's another in the fridge, if you want it.

Jake You've known Gilly, what?

Alex Oh . . .

Jake University.

Alex Twenty years.

Jake Did you ever . . .

Alex What? Gilly and I?

Jake Yes.

Alex Have you asked her that?

Jake No.

Alex Then why are you asking me?

Jake Just curious. Small c. What's this?

A box of twelve Durex sealed in a hard-plastic supermarket security pack.

Alex Sainsbury's delivery.

Jake You didn't nick 'em then?

Alex It's impossible to open.

Jake Condoms are safe then; pity about the sex.

Alex I could take a hammer to it, but I quite like it on the shelf. Installation art.

Jake Are you into that?

Alex Not really.

Jake Gilly dragged me to that Saatchi Gallery. Half a cow. Glass box of flies. Posh corniced room with oil on the floor. Black reflection in the oil as deep as the room was high. All a bit creepy, really. I never know where she'll drag me next.

Alex Welcome.

Jake Nothing personal.

Alex No pressure.

Jake None expected.

Alex Another?

Jake Thank you. So when did you decide orgies were The Way to Go?

Alex I had a lodger. Long time ago. She came over all confessional one evening. Told me her District Manager had taken her to a club. Said it was a bit of an eye-opener, but she enjoyed 'the vibe'. So the second time they went was a Wednesday and things were a bit quiet so apparently she and her District Manager put on a show.

Jake Put on a show?

Alex Put a show on. When you're the only ones at it and others are watching, that's . . . putting on a show.

Jake She put on a show with her District Manager?

Alex Yes.

Jake She didn't think that was a bit off?

Alex Obviously not. I presume she fancied him. I mean she wasn't after a pay hike or . . . East Croydon or anything.

Jake He sounds a bit dubious, though.

Alex I don't know him.

Jake I'd say he was chancing his arm.

Alex Well, right; but this was years ago.

Jake Ah.

Alex Before all that.

Jake Right.

Alex Back in the day.

Jake Pats on the bum.

Alex Mistletoe.

Jake Stationery cupboard.

Alex Photocopier.

Jake Sense of humour.

Alex Sense of proportion.

Jake I mean; that's where the vast majority of us *met*. Before it was entirely random.

Alex Swipe left?

Jake Married man.

Alex So the lodger said, 'You're curious, aren't you?' And I said, 'Of course I am.' And she said, 'He who desires and acts not breeds pestilence.' Well, I couldn't argue with that. So a month later Hetty and I are in the car and we're heading for a club next to a police station in Wednesbury.

Jake Sounds enticing.

Alex Little green door at the back of the place. You pay your money, you put your wine behind the bar.

Jake Bring your own?

Alex Well, you can't *sell* alcohol to people having sex, apparently, because that would be a disorderly house.

Jake Wouldn't want that.

Alex You get given a towel, go to the locker room.

Jake Any banter?

Alex Banter?

Jake Locker-room banter.

Alex It's not that sort of locker room.

Jake Oh.

Alex It's not a golf club, it's a . . .

Both . . . swingers' club.

Jake Right.

Alex Besides; it's unisex.

Jake The locker room?

Alex Yes. The men put on the towels. The women change into whatever they like. Lingerie, latex . . . whatever.

Jake Doesn't that . . .

Alex What?

Jake Spoil it a bit?

Alex It *is* a bit Tooting Lido, to be fair. But the club's nice in a West Midlands pub sort of a way. Banquets, little dance floor with a pole. Rooms to play in, rooms with the door closed, rooms with the door ajar, which is code for 'come in'. Windows you can watch through. Vinyl mattresses.

Jake Kinky.

Alex Easy to clean.

Jake Ah.

Alex Gruesome plaster grotto at the back, with a jacuzzi.

Jake Oh, no thanks.

Alex What?

Jake Bodily fluids.

Alex But the reassuring aroma of chlorine.

Jake That's not good.

Alex Hygiene's a thing.

Jake If the water's clean you can't smell the chlorine. If you can smell the chlorine then the chlorine's *working*, so there's stuff in the water it's working *on*.

    Pause.

Alex Really?

Jake Really.

Alex Oh.

Jake But you're a jacuzzi man?

Alex Well, I was.

Enter Hetty.

Hetty Man talk?

Alex Of course.

Hetty We're having girl talk.

Alex Of course you are.

Hetty And Gilly needs another. My mum called. She sends her love.

Alex That's nice.

Hetty She likes you. Dad not so much. He thinks you're too old for me.

Alex Why?

Hetty Because you're two years older than he is.

Hetty kisses Alex, then kisses Jake rather more extravagantly.
Exit Hetty with prosecco.

Alex Hetty's a bit old fashioned. In a good way.

Jake She seems . . . very nice.

Alex She is.

Jake And the . . . hygiene aspect of all this doesn't bother you at all?

Alex People are careful. I mean no one's *not* careful.

Jake I was just wondering.

Alex It won't affect you two.

Jake No. We certainly won't be clubbing in Wednesbury.

Alex It's a lot like being down the pub; except you haven't got your clothes on. And there's a dungeon downstairs.

Jake A w . . . d?

Alex Used to be the beer cellar.

Jake What constitutes a dungeon?

Alex A hobby horse and a plywood partition with holes in it.

Jake And all this turned you on, did it?

Alex Well, yes and no. It's sexy, but pedestrian. Hieronymus Bosch in Smethwick. Hetty and I found a little alcove with our Sauvignon.

Jake Sauvignon?

Alex I'm more a Picpoul man myself.

Jake I was going to say.

Alex But Hetty likes a Sauvignon.

Jake And you're a gentleman.

Alex I am. It wasn't bad, actually. Graham Norton's. It's dryer than some.

Enter Hetty.

Hetty I've lost my bubbles.

Alex Right there.

Jake I don't like Graham Norton.

Alex Don't you? I do.

Hetty I don't. I think he makes a mockery of Eurovision. Has he taken you through the Green Door? Is that where we are?

Jake Yes.

Hetty Has he told you about the PVC pole dancers?

Jake No.

Hetty Tell him about the PVC pole dancers.

Alex No.

Hetty Two girls, early twenties? Playing on the pole. They couldn't pole dance, they were just mucking about.

Alex They had on those terrible / PVC nurse's costumes.

Hetty PVC nurse's costumes. Ten quid on eBay. He liked the one with no knickers on. Didn't you? She was his favourite.

Jake No knickers?

Hetty She could *not have* cared less.

Jake That's quite sexy.

Hetty Which is what he said.

Alex Which is what I said. And then you said –

Hetty Then I said, 'Well, if it's turning you on, / have a wank.'

Alex 'Have a wank.'

Jake You said that?

Hetty And then he said . . .

Alex 'I can't just have a wank.'

Hetty And I said, 'Of course you can . . .'

Both 'It's a sex club.'

Jake So whhhat did you . . .

Alex So I put down my glass of Graham Norton . . .

Hetty Dropped his towel and had a wank.

Jake Did they notice?

Alex Yes, but they took no notice.

Hetty The tall one tried a bit harder.

Alex Did an upside-down thing and fell on her head.

Hetty Then what happened? What happened then?

Alex Well . . . out of the blue.

Hetty We barely knew each other.

Alex Hetty went down on me.

Hetty Hoorah for Hetty.

Alex Thank you very much.

Hetty Is this too much information?

Jake In any other circumstances, yes.

Alex The couple on the table next to us raise their glasses. My vision goes skew-whiff. My pupils dilate or something.

Hetty To cut a long story short . . .

Jake Not on my account.

Alex Frankly?

Hetty He came like a train.

Jake Blimey.

Alex What can I say? Sex in public. Whodathunk it?

Hetty Big grin on his face for the rest of the night.

Jake Wow.

Alex It wasn't just the towel I dropped. More like a heavy old greatcoat, caked in mud. Shame, that mud was. That's what dropped off my shoulders that night: my shame. Bit of a life-changer, really.

Hetty Thank you, Hetty.

Alex Thank you, Hetty.

Jake Well, I look forward to walking out of here a changed man.

Alex Well, you might.

Jake Don't expect too much of us.

Alex Nothing is expected of you.

Jake Either of us.

Enter Gilly.

Gilly Da da!

Hetty Da da!

Gilly (*Pink Panther*) Dadadadadadadadada daaaah dadadadada.

Alex That's terrific.

Gilly It's not too much?

Alex No.

Hetty Or too little?

Gilly It's *definitely* too little.

Jake You look great.

Gilly Thank you, kind sir.

Jake Come here, you.

Gilly Ooh. Forceful.

Jake kisses Gilly.

Hetty Ahh. Marital bliss.

Gilly That's us.

Jake Married alive.

Gilly Charming.

Alex As long as you're both on the same page.

Jake We've discussed it, yes.

Gilly We're definitely on the same page.

Alex Good.

Gilly Different books, same page.

Hetty Page sixty-nine.

Gilly That's a nice page. Jake prefers page ninety-six. That's how we sleep.

Doorbell.

Hetty Ouup. Here we go.

Gilly Oh my Gaaaahd.

Hetty Who's getting it?

Alex You get it.

Hetty I'll get it.

Alex Take off your dress and get it.

Hetty It's not a pizza.

Doorbell.
Lights.

SCENE TWO

9.00 p.m.
Music and conversation from the living room.
Alex, Jeff and Magdalena.

Jeff This is nice. You have a nice home. It's a nice crowd.

Magdalena Sweetheart, do you have tequila?

Alex We have vodka.

Magdalena No; we need some tequila.

Alex We don't have tequila.

Magdalena Is there a shop?

Alex I don't think so.

Magdalena You live here; we drive to a shop.

Alex I've been drinking.

Magdalena We both go. For tequila.

Jeff You don't need tequila.

Alex We have vodka?

Magdalena What sort of vodka?

Alex I don't know. It's in a skull.

Magdalena Then is not real vodka!

Alex Real enough, I should think.

Magdalena I would *LOVE* tequila.

Jeff You don't *need* tequila.

Magdalena I'll have a vodka. Skull vodka.

Jeff It's a very nice set-up you have here. Well done.

Alex Thank you.

Magdalena You have quirky taste. I have quirky taste. He has boring taste. He's American.

Alex How did you two meet?

Magdalena He was desperate.

Jeff We met in Gdansk.

Magdalena He was looking for sex.

Jeff She wasn't.

Magdalena I hate sex.

Jeff She was looking for a husband.

Magdalena I found one. Rich. Hoorah. American. Yawn. Do you have olives?

Alex Yes.

Magdalena I like it dirty.

Alex But you hate sex?

Magdalena I *LOVE* sex.

Jeff I'm an extremely lucky man; according to her.

Magdalena I was looking for love. But in wrong place; I find him instead. But he loves me. Don't you, darling?

Jeff Yes, I do.

Magdalena He hates to share me.

Jeff Breaks my heart.

Magdalena But I have to be free.

Jeff And married.

Magdalena Free to love.

Jeff She has to be both. Don't you?

Magdalena Yes.

Jeff I don't know how you feel, Alex, but we feel a couple needs a strong bond if they're going to play. There's nothing casual about being casual. I mean, you've got to know who you're going home with.

Magdalena And he is my home. He adores me.

Alex And you met in Gdansk?

Magdalena He won me in a poker game.

Jeff I don't remember it that way.

Magdalena How do you remember it?

Jeff I remember it as the night I almost lost a Maserati.

Alex What's your business?

Jeff Oh, import-export.

Magdalena Do no business with him. DO NOT GIVE HIM DETAILS OF YOUR BANK ACCOUNT. And DO NOT play poker, unless you can to win me off him. Please. You can try for me. I am very bored with him. But DO NOT BET YOUR GIRLFRIEND. Or you will lose.

Jeff We're not here to play poker.

Magdalena Ask him what he import-exports.

Alex I'm sure he'll tell me if he wants to.

Magdalena No. He will tell you a lie.

Alex Drugs, then.

Pause.

Jeff You got it.

Alex Drugs?

Jeff That okay?

Alex Obviously I'd draw the line at people.

Magdalena You see? Moral fibres!

Enter Hetty.

Hetty Alright, American Man. Do you mind if I call you that?

Jeff Is it a compliment?

Hetty I don't know yet.

Jeff My name's Jeff.

Hetty Was your grandad a cowboy?

Jeff No, he was on Wall Street.

Hetty Did he throw himself out of a window?

Jeff He may as well have.

Hetty Can I call you Geoffrey?

Jeff Just plain old Jeff.

Magdalena He will be very friendly, but don't be his friend. Just have sex with him; is best for you.

Hetty Alright. If you insist. Are you coming in, sweet?

Alex In a minute.

Hetty Are you alright?

Alex I'm fine.

She kisses him. Takes Jeff's hand.

Hetty Come on then, plain old Jeff. There's a party in the living room that needs livening up.

Jeff How could I refuse?

Exit Hetty and Jeff.

Magdalena Your girlfriend is the type of my husband likes. I am not this.

Alex Not what?

Magdalena I am type who husband like him marries. No complaining. Waste of time. When are you going to have sex?

Alex Oh, eventually.

Magdalena Who with, you intend?

Alex Anyone who'll have me, I suppose.

Magdalena Poor little lamb. Too much wolf's clothing I think. I have to have sex now. Would you like?

Alex Well . . .

Magdalena Do you have absinthe?

Alex No.

Magdalena No?

Alex Absinthe. Maybe later.

Magdalena Would you like to know my safe words?

Alex I need to know those, do I?

Magdalena Is best

Alex What are your safe words?

Magdalena 'Don't stop'.

Doorbell.

I will answer! Whoever is at door; I will have sex with them.

Exit Magdalena.
Lights.

SCENE THREE

10.00 p.m.
Alex uncovering the buffet.
Enter Gilly.

Gilly Well, it's all kicking off in there.

Alex Are you enjoying it?

Gilly I'm not not.

Alex Is Jake?

Gilly I think so. I wasn't sure he would.

Alex Why not?

Gilly You don't know Jake. He can be a bit uptight.

Alex Should you be keeping an eye on him, or are you deliberately not?

Gilly Neither. He'll stay in the corner where I left him. It's all a bit of an eye-opener, isn't it? I didn't expect quite so much . . . enthusiasm.

Alex But you're enjoying yourselves?

Gilly Yes, thank you. We've enjoyed ourselves already.

Alex Oh. I missed that.

Gilly Well, you're sitting in the kitchen.

Alex I'm shy.

Gilly I've noticed. We'll probably enjoy ourselves again later. You can watch.

Enter Tim.

Tim Wow.

Alex Wow what?

Tim Wow nothing. Just wow. Do you mind if I roll a spliff?

Alex You'll have to smoke it in the garden.

Tim Of course.

Alex There's a pond.

Tim Right.

Alex Don't fall in it.

Tim Righto.

Gilly How's it going in there?

Tim Magdalena's still at it.

Gilly She's pretty impressive.

Alex She is.

Tim She *really* likes fucking.

Alex She certainly does.

Gilly So what are you waiting for?

Alex A bit less momentum, I think.

Tim Pond.

   Exit Tim.

Gilly Jake's not up for anything other than he and I.

Alex That's why I said what I said.

Gilly For some reason he still thinks I'm gorgeous.

Alex You are gorgeous.

Gilly You'd think after fifteen years it would've worn off a bit, wouldn't you?

Alex You have an active sex life, then?

Gilly When we're not attending sex parties?

Alex When you're not attending sex parties.

Gilly Well, yes; we do.

Alex How many times a week?

Gilly Seven or eight.

Alex Seven or eight?

Gilly That's quite a lot, is it?

Alex Yes.

Gilly I thought it was. I bend over the bathroom sink and he's behind me. Are you enjoying *your*self, sitting in the kitchen?

Alex I like the kitchen.

Gilly Hetty's a bit of a goer.

Alex Yes, she is. On occasion. What's she up to?

Gilly She was . . . servicing the American.

Alex John.

Gilly Jeff.

Alex Jeff.

Gilly When I last saw her. She's very bubbly.

Alex Yes.

Gilly And quite / young.

Alex Young? She's thirty.

Gilly Don't get tetchy. Have you know her long?

Alex Years. I was queuing for a visa at the American Embassy. She offered me a jelly baby. I took her to Sheekey's.

Gilly How old was she then?

Alex Well, younger, obviously, as was I. There's a difference between young and too young. Which she isn't. And wasn't.

Gilly Honestly; your life.

Alex Yeh. I wonder where that went.

Gilly We are, aren't we? We're getting old.

Alex Speak for yourself. Only married people get old.

Gilly Ho. Ho. I mean that's what all this is about really, isn't it?

Alex I don't think so.

Gilly I do.

Alex I don't.

Gilly I know. You're only as young as the not very young –

Alex Perfectly appropriately aged person you feel.

Gilly You are such an arse.

Tim (*off*) Bit of a problem.

Alex What?

Enter Tim.

Tim Stepped in the pond.

Alex I warned you about that.

Tim Forgot. It's quite deep for a pond.

Gilly Have you hurt yourself?

Tim Lost my spliff.

Gilly You're sopping wet.

Tim No. Just from the waist down.

Gilly Take off your trousers.

Tim No, I'm fine.

Alex Take your trousers off.

Tim I suppose I could.

Gilly Of course you can.

Tim Wouldn't normally be appropriate, of course.

Gilly But under the circumstances.

Tim Thing is . . . I don't think Camilla wants to join in. If I walk in there with my trousers off she might think I'm being pushy.

Gilly She seems happy enough; watching.

32

Tim Do you think?

Gilly She's even made the odd suggestion.

Tim She's a goddess.

Gilly She's pretty confident.

Tim Isn't she? A bloody goddess.

Gilly A bit opinionated, maybe.

Tim She is. She is. Wonderful woman.

Alex Are you on drugs?

Tim I like drugs.

Alex I know you do.

Tim You don't like them. I know that. We've talked about that.

Alex I don't like the way they divorce dickheads like you from reality.

Tim That's what I *do* like about them. You should try some MDMA.

Gilly Don't.

Alex I'd go paranoid. I'd see undercover police everywhere. Then I'd turn into a mushroom.

Tim All that happens very rarely. Go on. You'll never look back.

Alex Some people never *get* back.

Tim I do. Invariably. I'm back the next morning.

Gilly And you feel okay?

Tim Well, no, actually. I feel shit until Thursday.

Alex I'm looking you straight in the eye.

Tim Right.

Alex And you're not really there.

Tim I know. Isn't that great?

Alex No, it's not great.

Tim Well, I feel great.

Alex Do you?

Tim Yes.

Gilly *Do* you?

Tim Absolutely.

Alex Well, you don't look it. I feel like locking you in a bedroom.

Tim How do I look?

Alex Like a bewildered corpse.

Tim That's EXACTLY it. Bewildered, but at the same time, pretty sure of myself.

He looks at himself in the mirror.

A bit corpse-like, but fucking immortal, also. Seriously. You should try some. It's not a pattern is it, around this mirror; it's writing. You see, that's the opposite of psychosis. A psychotic would see a pattern and think it's writing. I saw writing and thought it was a pattern. 'I change. I stay the same. I change. I stay the same.' Who wrote that then?

Gilly Leonard Cohen wrote it. He wrote it round Marianne's mirror.

Tim 'So Long, Marianne' Marianne?

Alex Yes.

Tim Wow. So you wrote it round your mirror.

Alex Well. Someone did.

Tim Cool. I dig it.

Gilly So did I.

Alex Why do people talk like bloody hippies when they're on drugs?

Tim I know! They do, don't they. I've noticed that.

Alex *And* there's something in drugs that makes you talk exclusively about drugs.

Tim And something else that makes you question your entire existence.

Gilly Mopping the kitchen floor has much the same effect on me.

Tim Seriously?

Gilly Seriously.

Tim You're not being serious. I'm being serious. The whole existential question. On the cab ride over here. Why are we here? What's the meaning of life? I know it sounds stupid but it's bloody profound.

Alex These are thoughts that lots of people have. They have them when they're *not* on MDMA. *You*, Tim, only have them when you *are* on MDMA.

Tim And it's all-consuming! But at the same time, and here's the thing about mandy, at the same time . . . you don't give a fuck. About any of it. That's the thing. That's why I take the stuff.

Alex I see.

Tim You see?

Alex I do.

Tim But what?

Alex Well . . .

Tim You see. I knew there was a but. How did I *know* that?

Alex Tim: *no one* gives a damn. We question our existence and we don't give a fuck. That's not just you; that's all of us.

Gilly That's a bit cynical.

Tim That's the point; it's impossible to be cynical if you're on a bit of molly-mandy. That's the point I've been trying to make.

Gilly It's very hard to talk to you when your pupils are so big.

Tim Would you like one?

Alex No, she would not. I've seen her at Christmas.

Tim You know, I never thought I'd find the perfect woman. There's always something they don't like about me. Camilla's happy with the Scotch and the weed; the pills not so much. Otherwise she's perfect. She's a bloody goddess. I'm going to ask her if I can take my trousers off.

Alex You never know your luck.

Exit Tim.

He should never have moved to Brighton.

Gilly How many years? You and me?

Alex Twenty? Since we fucked, you mean?

Gilly No! Since we met.

Alex Twenty-one, two? That was a very emphatic 'no'.

Gilly Because we never did.

Alex Didn't we?

Gilly No, we didn't.

Alex Yes we did. Back of the wool shop.

Gilly Nope. I sucked you off.

Alex My head in the cashmere. I thought we fucked.

Gilly I know we didn't because I remember telling myself we wouldn't.

Alex I could have sworn we did. We *slept* together.

Gilly We shared the bed.

Alex So why didn't we?

Gilly Well, I was being pretty promiscuous at the time. That's probably why not.

Alex Ah. Story of my life. Chapter One.

Gilly Hetty seems very . . .

Alex Very what?

Gilly Obedient.

Alex No, no no. She just enjoys being told what to do.

Gilly So she's a . . . submissive?

Alex Only when she *chooses* to be.

Gilly Well, I should hope so.

Alex She's a dab hand with a leather paddle.

Gilly I don't want to know.

Alex Me neither. Once was enough.

Gilly Alex; she *snogged me*.

Alex Did you like that?

Gilly Jake did. I think. I mean I asked and he said 'go ahead'. I suppose girls don't count.

Alex Obviously not. Did you like it?

Gilly She certainly enjoys being the centre of attention.

Alex But do you *like* her?

Gilly Is she being herself, or is she being who you want her to be?

Alex I don't really understand what you're saying but I think I'm being got at.

Gilly Yes you are, so yes, you do. When you told her to . . .

Alex Do what I told her to doodley-do.

Gilly My mouth fell open. I didn't realise mouths actually did that. I'd always thought that was just bad comedy acting, but no; it fell open. I had to close it again.

Alex Hetty's attitude to sex is simple: anyone in the room who wants it . . . deserves it.

Gilly That's hardly simple.

Alex I mean, she feels that in the pub, frankly. Let alone a party.

Gilly That's insane.

Alex That's Hetty. She can be very choosy but she prefers to be chosen. She sacrifices her right to choose on the Altar of Choice.

Gilly And you never get jealous?

Alex Sometimes. But no.

Gilly Jake would. That's why we daren't. Do people you know, *know*?

Alex Some.

Gilly Are they impressed or appalled?

Alex Intrigued, mostly.

Gilly To your face, maybe. But what do they say behind your back?

Alex I don't know. What will *you* say; at your next coffee morning?

Gilly Nothing, obviously. I'm sitting in the kitchen and my dress is in the living room.

Enter Hetty.

Hetty WHAT are you doing in the *kitchen*?

Gilly Gossiping. What are you doing in the living room?

Hetty What happens in the living room / stays in the living room.

Gilly Stays in the living room. Like my husband. Who at most parties is invariably to be found *in the kitchen*.

Hetty Well, tonight it's the living room.

Gilly I can't imagine why.

Enter Jeff.

Jeff Great party. Good people. Nice ambience.

Hetty That man . . . has got a very nice dick.

Jeff Thank you.

Gilly What are your criteria?

Hetty Oh, it's either thumbs up or thumbs down, really.

Gilly Size doesn't matter then?

Hetty Good God no; size doesn't matter.

Gilly Size doesn't matter, Alex.

Hetty Size doesn't matter, Greg.

Jeff Jeff.

Alex Well, I wouldn't know, obviously.

Gilly The only time size matters is if you forget to say size doesn't matter.

Hetty Or when it's toooo big.

Gilly Oh, yes; all those times.

Alex Please; my ears are burning.

Jeff May I make a suggestion?

Alex Go ahead.

Gilly What?

Jeff I think *you* should come into the living room and seduce your husband.

Gilly Why?

Jeff So's I can watch.

Pause.

Gilly Alright, then.

Pause.

If you touch me he'll chin you.

Jeff I shall sit on the far side of the room. You throw a great party.

Alex Wait till you see the buffet.

Exit Gilly, followed by Jeff.

Hetty Are you cross?

Alex What about?

Hetty Are you okay?

Alex I'm fine.

Hetty You're not. I know you're not. Why are you sitting in the kitchen?

Alex I'm thinking.

Hetty Thinking what?

Alex Well, if you must know, I was wondering what we were all doing here.

Hetty We're having a party.

Alex I was being philosophical.

Hetty Why are you being philosophical? You took a Viagra and shaved your scrotum. Why are you being philosophical NOW? What's the matter? I know when something's the matter.

Alex Nothing's the matter.

Hetty This is what you were like that Christmas. People get merry and you get moribund.

Enter Magdalena.

Magdalena Stupid skull is empty. Was good vodka. I know vodka.

Alex Good, was it?

Magdalena Not Russian, but not Polish. You have fucked me yet?

Alex No. My sincere apologies. I'm waiting till you're back in the stadium.

Magdalena Sometimes I not even look. Once, I fall asleep; ha! Am too greedy. Not care. Why you not fucking *her*?

Alex Henrietta and I have all the time in the world.

Hetty That's what he thinks!

Magdalena The one with husbandy husband? You should fuck her. Is your party; why not? I know. Not to worry. I not have fucked him. But if you want, I will; then you could fuck *her*.

Hetty They seemed happy enough together in the corner.

Magdalena No. She not happy. Our husbands; they talk on sofa. Engineering. Electricals. Yawn. She's unhappy woman. Very nice house. Nice people. The one in big armchair a bit bossy. But imaginative. And the quiet one is quiet. I think she's here because her boyfriend. Good vodka. Stupid bottle. I think of death very much. We have a house. His house; we have it. In the country of Dev-on. In the winter we are not there, it gets cold, we arrive for weekend – below zero. I know; you are Russian, you say; but I hate the cold. So, there is an Aga. I call it the Agaaaagh. You have to crawl to light it and it will not light and I am on hands and knees in a rabbit coat – he says mink but pah – is rabbit. On my knees to light this Agaaaagh. Then a night and day for the house to warm. But that is not the point I want to say. We sit freezing, only three channels on the television, and slowly house warms up and this is the point I wanted to say. There is one time . . . a butterfly. And one Christmas, 'half the dozen'? They flew in of the summer and then they, I don't know, they hide away and it grows cold and you think they would die, no? A butterfly so cold. You see it hanging on the curtain and you think: dead butterfly. In the bathroom corner, dead butterfly. But no. No, no. You hear: flutter flutter flutter. And the first time you think WHAT ON HELL is that. And then you see. One Christmas; like baubles on the tree but in the air, fluttering around. Was beautiful. I know. You think I'm hard bitch – everyone thinks I'm hard bitch because I like to be fucked but these butterflies, they touch my heart. So small, so patient, so pretty. And sometimes in morning I wake to the flutter and I go to window, and there is lonely butterfly against the glass, flapping to go outside. But outside is cold, I tell it. Inside is warm, outside is freeze to death. But it doesn't know; is desperate to go, God knows where. And I put my hand on window handle and I think I let it go outside where it thinks is life and sun and flowers and other butterflies and butterfly sex – it thinks whole life is out there and inside is nothing. Warm world that is life is the world it doesn't want. World it wants is cold world that kill it . . . People think I am hard bitch. And think I don't think. Because I think Russian and talk English. They think I think . . . not deep . . .

Hetty They think you're shallow.

Magdalena Shallow! Yes, they think, but no. All these thoughts I have from just one butterfly.

Hetty Are you the butterfly?

Magdalena You know? I think yes. Once I was. Not any more. You want to fuck me now? It will stop me talking.

Enter Camilla and Tim.

Camilla Do you have a tumble dryer?

Alex Next to the fridge.

Tim Thanks.

Camilla It's a mystery to me; what I see in you.

Tim You said I've got a lot more potential than most men.

Camilla Comic potential, maybe.

Alex Twiddle the thing and press the blue button.

Tim Right.

Enter Gilly and Jake.

Gilly It was only a suggestion.

Jake Yes; but whose? Can I get another beer?

Alex Unless you'd like some crack.

Jake You've got . . .?

Both Ha haaah.

Jake Had me there.

Camilla May I make an observation?

Alex Of course.

Camilla May I?

Alex Yes, you may.

43

Camilla It's just an observation.

Alex Which suggests quite possibly it isn't.

Camilla That's all it is.

Alex I'm intrigued.

Camilla There are no black people at this party.

Alex Ah.

Camilla Don't you know any black people?

Alex Yes, I do.

Hetty Yes; he does. So do I.

Camilla They just happen not to be here?

Alex Lots of people I know happen not to be here. I can't imagine why.

Camilla Did you invite any black people?

Alex No.

Camilla So how many black people do you know?

Alex Lots.

Camilla How many?

Alex Er . . . Three.

Camilla Is that all?

Alex Plus the pub. How many *should* I know?

Camilla You see, that's a very strange way to talk about people.

Alex Is it? Was I?

Camilla The point is . . .

Alex Yes, Ms Kuenssberg; what *is* the point?

Camilla Why are there no black people at your party?

Magdalena Or Gypsies!

Alex Gypsies?!

Camilla Why not?

Magdalena Bad idea. Would steal stuff.

Alex Which is why I didn't invite any, obviously.

Tim Well, actually, I did the Glastonbury clean-up with some Gypsies. They were cool, actually.

Hetty Would anybody like another striptease?

Alex Good try, Hetty. No thanks. I don't make invites on a quota system.

Camilla No black people, no gay people. Not even a bisexual.

Gilly Well, hello.

Jake You don't count.

Gilly Why not?

Jake Because you weren't when you got here.

Gilly Oh.

Alex So, you seem to be suggesting I'm a racist homophobe?

Tim No; she's not. It's just the way she talks.

Camilla Unconsciously, perhaps.

Hetty Well, I don't like the way she talks.

Alex I know black people. I once saw a gay bloke across the street. I'm even on speaking terms with a trans person!

Hetty Frozen Meals Man!

Alex Chap goes in the corner shop. We always say hi.

Hetty Not a chap, though.

Alex No. Wig and handbag equals woman.

Tim Right. I bet shopping's a bitch.

Camilla Textbook transphobia.

Alex That's what I was attempting. But phobia's not the right word, even if I was, which I'm not.

Camilla Who are you to say that?

Alex Someone who's not afraid. Spiders, maybe. People: fear's not it. Prejudice maybe, but I'm not that either.

Camilla All I'm saying . . .

Alex I know what you're saying. And with respect, I'm shutting you down.

Tim Now, now.

Alex Down, not up. Look, these things are traditionally straight. I'm straight, so I threw a party, and it's straight.

Camilla And white.

Alex It *happens* to be white, yes.

Camilla Just happens to be white.

Alex So which shall we cancel, me or it?

Gilly You know, I've known Alex half of my life. And he's none of those things.

Alex I'm really not.

Camilla I apologise. I sometimes smell hypocrisy where there is none. Have I put my foot in it? I have, haven't I? People don't like straight talking. That's why I like Tim. Tim has no pretence about him. That's why I love Tim. But I do tend to go off on one. So I apologise.

Exit Camilla.

Tim It's just the way she talks.

Pause.

Gilly Jake.

Jake What?

Gilly Come into the living room.

Jake Why?

Gilly I've had an idea. All of my own.

She kisses him. They leave.
Magdalena and Alex are left alone. They look at each other.
Lights.

SCENE FOUR

10.15 p.m.
Jake and Alex.

Jake So; you're in bed with someone. Well, with Gilly.

Alex Of course.

Jake You love them, you like them, a one-night stand, whatever, whoever. But in my case Gilly, and you're having sex, and there's this voice in your head. 'The car won't start. Is it the battery or the alternator? That prick at work; should I placate him or draw the line? Should I cancel Netflix or Now TV? There's nothing left I want to see on either. Is Scarlett Johansson pretty? Or just, you know? If both sets of parents descend on Sunday, would a barbecue be easier?' It never shuts up.

Alex I know that voice.

47

Jake It's not even that annoying. I mean, these are all things that need thinking about. But it dulls the event somewhat.

Alex And that other voice, too.

Jake Another voice?

Alex 'Is she into it tonight or is she faking it?'

Jake Oh, that voice! 'Would she like me to slow down or just get it over with? Is this the only woman . . .'

Both '. . . I will ever make love to?'

Jake Constant fucking earache. Anyway. You grow used to that, and eventually . . . that's what sex is.

Alex I understand.

Jake Until tonight. Until just then. I was having sex with my wife half an hour ago, with that American watching, and whatsisname . . .

Alex Tim.

Jake Playing with himself, and all of a sudden . . . I was fucking my wife and for the first time in, I don't know, for*ever* . . . that's all I was doing. There were no voices, no inane chattering in my head. In a room full of strangers, it was just . . . Gilly and I.

Alex What did I tell you?

Jake Not an ounce of privacy, and there we were; alone at last.

Alex Sounds great.

Jake How bloody paradoxical is that?

Alex I'm seriously considering taking up counselling full time.

Jake It was intense.

Alex Focused.

Jake It really was.

Alex Bit of a life-changer, eh?

Jake You know, I think so.

Alex Fancy a swap, then?

Jake Fuck off.

Pause. Alex gets a drink.

Did you mean that or were you just . . .?

Alex I was just. I often just. Then I just.

Jake She and Hetty seem to be getting on.

Alex How do you feel about that?

Enter Gilly.

Gilly Someone spilt something.

Alex Red or white?

Gilly Red.

Alex Oh fuck. What on? The Persian. Of course. Where else.

Alex finds the salt and exits.

Gilly Refill, please. Happier now?

Jake Yes. You?

Gilly Super, thanks.

He fills her glass.

Jake So. Are you bisexual from now on?

Gilly Definitely. That okay?

Jake Fine by me.

Pause.

Gilly You know, you can if you want.

Jake Can what?

Gilly Whatever. Whoever. I don't mind if you do.

Jake I don't want to.

Gilly Do you mind that I don't mind?

Jake Is that a trick question?

Gilly No. It's a generous one.

Jake Is it?

Gilly Well if it isn't, what is it?

Jake It's a very strange question, that's all.

Gilly I'm not being strange, or odd, or devious . . . I just want you to know that tonight, if you want to whatever, then I'm okay with that. Tonight was on your bucket list, right? Well, here we are. In the bucket.

Jake And what about you?

Gilly What about me?

Jake Well, you're in the bucket too.

Gilly Oh you mean, do I want to . . . whatever?

Jake Fuck someone else.

Gilly Not . . . specifically.

Jake Specifically?

Gilly Particularly. Specifically. Either. Both.

Jake I love a straight answer.

Gilly If you mean if I, meaning you, did, and you were, and you looked over your shoulder, would I be at it with whoever, then no; I wouldn't be.

Jake Then what's in it for you?

Gilly I think I'd like to watch. I'd like to see you happy.

Jake As opposed to when?

Gilly As opposed to hardly ever.

Enter Alex.

Alex Panic's over.

Gilly Jolly good.

Pause.

Alex There was a pause. Fire-pit might need a bit of attention, said Alex.

Gilly Keep the home fires burning.

Exit Alex.

Jake So I get to be unfaithful and you'd get to watch.

Gilly If you'd *like* that, yes.

Jake That's exceedingly generous.

Gilly No more than usual. We eat what you fancy, we watch what you want. Jalfrezi; *Game of Thrones*; these things hold no sway over me, but they are what we choose. All aspects of our cohabitation are an attempt to make you happy. This is our usual mode of existence. It's only the bucket that's different.

Jake You take no pleasure?

Gilly I take it where I can find it.

Jake Have you got a bucket list?

Gilly No. I've got a fuck-it list. Skydiving? No, thanks. Machu Picchu? With *my* knee? Dolphins, for Christ's sake. Fuck it.

Jake When did you make that up?

Gilly Hoovering, at a guess.

Jake Why haven't I heard it?

Gilly Because you wouldn't have laughed.

Jake Yes, I would; I just did.

Gilly No, you didn't.

Jake We can leave if you like.

Gilly I want you to enjoy yourself.

Jake And if I said you could if you wanted to, would you want to?

Gilly I would if you told me I *had* to.

Jake Clever answer.

Gilly I thought so.

Jake Well then; do what you like.

Gilly Oh . . .

Jake It's fine by me.

Gilly Let's not have a domestic.

Jake In the middle of a swingers party? I'm sure that wouldn't be a first.

Gilly Alright, let's go home. Do you want to go home?

Jake Do you want to fuck Alex?

Gilly Why would I . . . want to do that?

Jake Well, you seem pretty thick.

Gilly We're old friends.

Jake Are you sure?

Gilly Yes I'm sure. Are you not?

Jake Would you say no?

Gilly As in 'I wouldn't say no'?

Jake Yes.

Gilly No. I mean yes.

Jake You wouldn't say no or . . . no, you would say no.

Gilly I wouldn't say no, I suppose. Is that the same as yes?

Jake Of course it is.

Gilly It isn't really.

Jake Yes it is.

Gilly Alright! Yes. I wouldn't say no.

Jake Thank you. The answer was patently obvious.

Gilly Then why did I hesitate?

Jake I don't know; why did you?

Gilly I don't know.

Enter Alex.

Alex Blazing nicely.

Jake Love a good fire-pit.

Gilly You can't have one.

Jake Why not?

Gilly Your youngest child's a pyromaniac.

Alex Do you know what? I declare the buffet open.

Gilly Good. I'm ravenous.

Variously, they attack the buffet.
Enter Hetty and Magdalena.

Hetty We've decided we're going to be lesbians.

Magdalena Too many cocks. Too much men.

Hetty More fizz, Mags?

Magdalena Mags. I love to be Mags. I have never been called this. Now I am Mags. I love this.

Enter Jeff.

Magdalena Darling; I am Mags from now on. I answer to no other.

Jeff I'll make a note of that.

Doorbell.

Hetty I'll get it.

Magdalena Hurry back to your Mags; we shall lope together far away. (*To Gilly.*) You must come with us. I think you are a lesbian too.

Gilly I used to think I had tendencies, but it was just Elmhurst.

Magdalena You, definitely. She definitely!

Jake I don't think so.

Gilly I think she's right. It's been lovely, Jake, but I have to change my life.

Magdalena We shall live on Greek island.

Gilly Or in Camden. With cats.

Magdalena Lots of little pussies.

Jeff Good riddance to the lot of you, that's what I say.

Magdalena Because you are homo-thing.

Jeff I wish I was. The lifestyle would have suited me. But I'm not.

Enter Tim and Camilla from the garden.

54

Tim I put my wine down somewhere.

Camilla You don't need it.

Tim No, but it's a mystery.

Alex holds up a soggy red tea towel.

Alex Is this it?

Tim No; it was in a glass.

Alex What's wrong with your hand?

Camilla Run it under the tap.

Tim Marshmallows. Yum. Ouch.

Gilly Ooh, sugar, nasty.

Camilla He'll live.

Enter Hetty with Lucy.
One by one, the room look at her.

Hetty Alex; your new best friend is here.

Alex Lucy! Hi.

Lucy Hello.

Alex You came.

Lucy I came. I almost didn't, then I did.

Hetty Can I take your coat?

Lucy Thank you. Yes. I wasn't sure what to bring. I brought this.

Alex No need. Thank you. Let me introduce you. Jeff, Lucy, Lucy, Jeff. Magdalena, Lucy, Jake . . .

Jake My wife.

Hetty Hetty.

Gilly I'm Gilly.

Jake I said that.

Alex Camilla and Tim.

Tim Hi.

Lucy Hello.

Camilla Welcome.

Alex I'd take you through, but the party seems to be in the kitchen.

Lucy All the best parties are.

Jeff Except the ones enjoyed upon the ocean against a sinking Caribbean sun. And may I just say: you look absolutely fabulous.

Pause.

Lucy Thank you. Could I use your bathroom?

Alex Of course.

Hetty It's upstairs. I'll show you.

Lucy Thank you.

Exit Hetty and Lucy.

Camilla Tim, eyes back in their sockets, if you don't mind.

Tim Were they? Was I? Sorry.

Gilly She's *very* attractive.

Alex I thought so. And she's nice.

Gilly I'm sure.

Alex She's very nice.

Gilly And tall. Jake likes tall women.

Jake And short ones.

Camilla Louboutin.

Tim More the merrier!

Jake Alex, you have terrific taste.

Alex Thank you. I think.

Magdalena No, no no. She is man.

Alex She's what?

Magdalena She is man. In a dress.

Camilla You can't say that.

Tim Called Lucy?

Alex I don't think so.

Magdalena A man called Lucy.

Alex Lucy, yes. I mean I don't think she's . . . you think?

Jeff Well, is she or isn't she?

Enter Hetty.

Hetty A man called Lucy?

Jake Terrible western.

Gilly Shush.

Magdalena Is no problem.

Alex Look, I'm pretty sure Lucy isn't . . . I mean . . .

Jeff Where'd you two meet?

Hetty In Coco de Mer.

Jeff Well then; what did you expect? You sure?

Magdalena Man.

Camilla Trans woman, if you don't mind.

Hetty Well, how well do you know him?

Camilla Her.

Hetty Well, whoever he is, she is?

Jeff You have a thing for transsexuals?

Gilly Is that the word?

Jeff What month is it?

Alex What do you mean, a thing?

Camilla Alex, I'm pleasantly surprised. I owe you an apology, and that's not something I often say.

Tim No; that's a first, really.

Alex I haven't got a thing. Or a thing. Either way, I mean.

Gilly So is he a man in a dress called Lucy or is he *Lucy* in a dress?

Jake That doesn't make sense.

Gilly I mean there's a difference between *was* and *is*, moron.

Magdalena Well, you must ask him.

Alex Her.

Magdalena Him. Her.

Hetty So she's a *woman* in a dress?

Magdalena . . . yes.

Hetty What if she wasn't in a dress?

Magdalena Then a man, I think.

Tim Blimey.

Jake More tea, vicar?

Gilly Are we supposed to *know*?

Alex I don't know. I mean, I don't even know.

Camilla Well, presumably, she'd prefer to pass.

Gilly So do we *know* or do we *not* know?

Jake This is why I leave the room when you're doing a crossword.

Magdalena The best parties – there is always a pervert.

Hetty You can't say that!
Gilly You can't say that!
Camilla You can't say that!
Alex You can't say that!

Magdalena No, no; is a good thing.

Alex Alright, alright. I admit, some clarification *would* be welcome. I mean, is . . .

Tim She
Hetty She
Camilla She.

Alex Lucy. I mean who *is* she . . . is a perfectly valid question.

Jeff I'm glad you agree.

Enter Lucy. Silence.

Lucy Hello, again.

Alex Hi, Lucy.
Hetty Hello, Lucy
Gilly Lucy; hi.
Jake Lucy. Hello.
Jeff Lucy?
Tim Hiya Luce.
Camilla Lucy! Such a lovely name!
Magdalena Lucy, whatever.

Alex Let me get you a drink. What would you like? There's, well, just about everything.

Magdalena There is no tequila.

Jeff Or vodka.

Alex Fizz?

Magdalena Is prosecco.

Lucy Marvellous. I'd love some.

Alex I knew it. Lucy's a prosecco.

Pause.

Lucy So.

Hetty So. Welcome.

Alex Welcome, welcome, welcome.

Lucy Thank you. It probably goes without saying but there *is* something you should all know.

They all speak simultaneously.

Gilly Really?
Jake Hmm?
Tim What's that then?
Camilla . . . really no need.
Jeff And what might that be?
Magdalena We know, darling, we know.

Lucy This is my first sex party.

Gilly Oh. Us too.
Tim Absolutely. Same for us.
Camilla Well, apparently they're all the rage.
Jeff Well, well.
Magdalena We have been to many. Many, many, many.
Jake And our last.

Alex Well; first-timers, or vanilla people as we like to call them, are very welcome.

Lucy Thank you. And do you all know each other?

Alex More or less. I think everyone knows me, at least.

Hetty We're getting to know one another.

Gilly We certainly are.

Jake She certainly is.

Lucy So you're all . . . 'swingers'.

Gilly Oh, no.
Jake Nope.
Hetty Hardly.
Camilla I'm not.
Alex Guilty.

Jeff Sure.

Magdalena Definite, we are. We are international. Lots of invites, always. Copenhagen, South of France; but we love London. Is-ling-ton. The best place. Fabulous.

Camilla Really? Are you entirely sure of that?

Jeff I have a question. You said you almost didn't come. So why did you?

Lucy Well . . . I've always been curious.

Hetty Big C or little c?
Gilly Big C or little c?

Lucy Oh, strictly lower case. Some of us lead simple, quiet lives. I've always presumed the sex-positive to be a very exotic species.

Alex Are we what you expected?

Lucy Well, I hadn't imagined you all in the kitchen. But yes. More or less.

Gilly Ooh. More or less.

Jake Which of us is which?

Alex There are some languid souls in the living room.

Lucy Ah. Yes. I'd imagined something . . . livelier.

Hetty We were lively earlier.

Gilly You were exceedingly lively.

Hetty I know. Alex thinks I might be a nymphomaniac.

Jake I think he might be right.

Hetty Well, I don't. 'Cause I'm not. But I do love cocks. His included. Haven't seen yours.

Jeff What is it you love about them?

Hetty What I love *most* about cocks is they NEVER look like they belong to the man they belong to. It's like choosing a dog at Battersea. The man never thinks, well I'm small and cute so I'll choose the small and cute one; no, they want the big jumpy up one that'll see off burglars. And the tall handsome bloke falls for the pudgy little funny one, and that's what he's stuck with.

Jeff What's your opinion, Luce?

Lucy I love dogs.

Gilly Do you? I do. We went to Battersea last weekend.

Jake And the one before that.

Hetty Oh; did it break your heart?

Gilly We've always had a dog. Then Mabel died, so . . .

Hetty I'd love a dog. I miss my dog.

Gilly You're a dog person.

Hetty Oh, I am.

Lucy So am I.

Gilly I knew you were.

Hetty Alex isn't.

Alex I'm indifferent. Or allergic. Depends on the dog.

Jake I'm a dog person; she put a bed down for me in the kitchen.

Hetty Are *you* a dog person?

Jeff I thought we were talking about my penis.

Camilla We changed the subject.

Jeff Well, no; I'm not.

Hetty Oh, I am.

Jeff Why?

Hetty Because I LOVE DOGS.

Jeff I don't like dogs.

Lucy How can you not like dogs?

Jeff What's to like?

Lucy Dogs are loyal, dogs love you unconditionally.

Jeff I don't think they do.

Hetty Oh, they do.

Lucy Yes, they do.

Hetty They really do.

Jake Woof.

Jeff Dogs want to eat. They follow you to the kitchen because they want to eat. They sit up when you open the cookies; because they want to eat. They chase a rabbit; they want to eat it. They chase a ball for practice because they didn't catch the rabbit. You get home from Iraq, they go crazy; they think you went for food. They lick your hand for the *salt* and your face in the hope you'll vomit. They nuzzle the baby because they're *thinking* about it. Dogs want to eat. That's all dogs want.

Gilly That is so . . . I want to say cynical but it's not a good enough word.

Jake And it doesn't fit with two down.

Hetty Dogs are THE MOST LOVING creatures.

Jeff Because you *feed* them. Try not feeding them. And don't die alone in the house, because your dog will love you more each meal time.

Hetty My friend had a friend who died. His dog went to the graveyard every day and sat on the grave.

Jeff Because that's where they put the bones!

Hetty Have you ever watched two dogs playing together in the park?

Jeff Oh, they want sex too. They pee on the post-box; they're looking for sex. They sniff another dog's arse; they're looking for sex. They sniff your arse; they're looking for sex. They go apeshit if you say 'walkies'; they're desperate for sex. Food and sex. And a preference for sleeping indoors, it goes without saying.

Lucy There are times my dog just looks at me . . .

Jeff For *food*.

Hetty You've got a dog.

Lucy I do. If I'm depressed she lays her little chin in my lap.

Jeff And you give it a biscuit.

Hetty I lied. You've got a horrible dick. I planted carrots once. Only one came up. And it was like your dick.

Jeff I'm not saying you didn't love your dog.

Lucy Well, thank you.

Jeff I'm just saying *it* didn't love *you*.

64

Gilly Well; is there any *need* to say that?

Jeff You provided food, shelter and territorial support. Therefore it was loyal. It obeyed you. Because not to do so would be a Darwinian error.

Lucy Well, I don't care. I love my dog.

Jeff Because it provides you with an illusory sense of non-aloneness. Of being loved when of course you are not. The evidence for which would surely be your channelling of love in the direction of a fucking dog.

Hetty I was going to suck your root vegetable dick again but now I'm not.

Gilly Neither am I.

Alex Me neither. Sorry, Jeff. That was a sure thing and you blew it.

Jake Were you intending to?

Gilly What?

Magdalena Why *are* we in the kitchen?

Alex Because we're not on Antigua.

Magdalena There should be sex, yes? So who would like to fuck?

Jeff *Play.*

Magdalena Play. He likes me to say play.

Jeff The *word* is '*play*'.

Magdalena (*to Jake*) You should play with (*Re: Hetty.*) her. (*To Gilly.*) And you should play with (*Re: Alex.*) him. (*To Alex.*) She would like to play with you.

Gilly We're just old friends.

Jake We'll pass. Thank you.

Magdalena But if you let her fuck him you can fuck me. And her. You can fuck all of us. Admit it. You want to fuck her.

Jeff Could you keep your damn potty mouth shut for one damned minute.

Magdalena Ooph. Macho Man.

Camilla Typical cis-male.

Tim I'm one of those, apparently.

Alex Listen. I love you all, except those I don't know and those I don't, but I have a burden of care that I happily carry, so please: not in my house.

Jeff Well, sure. But are we going to DISCUSS this, or not? I don't mean to be offensive but these affairs are traditionally *heterosexual*.

   Lights.
      End of Act One.

Act Two

Continuous.

Lucy Traditionally heterosexual?

Jeff That's how this evening started out; yes.

Lucy And in what way is this evening no longer that?

Jeff Well, that's what I'm asking.

Camilla What precisely do you *mean* by heterosexual?

Jeff What do you mean what do I mean?

Magdalena We throw a party, he says, 'Only straight women and men to the party.'

Jeff I said no such thing.

Magdalena And lesbians, of course. He likes lesbians.

Jeff I have no particular prejudice.

Magdalena Good for the goose, good for the gander.

Jeff What I'm *saying* is . . . and I mean no offence, but if we were looking for something transgressive, well . . . we've done that; we've attended places where anything goes.

Magdalena 'Say goodbye to Mr Gnome.'

Hetty Who's Mr Gnome? Where did he go?

Magdalena You don't want to know. I can never not see that again.

Jeff Lucy; I'm as liberal as the next man . . .

Lucy But not when he reaches for your penis.

67

Jeff You see? We talk the same language.

Lucy I'm not entirely sure that's true.

Camilla Unfortunately for those of us who believe passionately in inclusivity, we often have to endure the attitudes of those who do not.

Jeff I just think it's incumbent on the host to ensure the guests are fully conversant with the inclinations of the other guests and that these things are usually considered *heterosexual* unless otherwise stated.

Alex Then consider it otherwise stated, and apologise.

Lucy There's no need.

Jeff I'm happy to apologise.

Magdalena Always happy to. Never does.

Alex Please. The buffet. It's a mixed selection of Waitrose and Iceland. I thought that might be an accurate reflection of the guest list. Joking. Not really. Tuck in.

Pause.

Hetty I love your perfume.

Lucy Krigler Oud.

Hetty I hate you.

Lucy It was a gift.

Hetty It's really unusual. Musky.

Lucy Some find it exotic, others find it taints the very air they breathe.

Hetty Well, I like it.

Jeff If it's me you're alluding to, I don't appreciate that.

Alex No one's alluding to anyone.

68

Jeff But for the record: I am NOT a transphobe.

Hetty He didn't say that.

Camilla Dear Lord.

Hetty She didn't. No one said that. Sorry.

Pause.

Lucy Perhaps I should go.

Hetty No! Please don't.

Alex Hetty gets muddled.

Hetty *Game of Thrones* – clueless.

Alex A slip of the tongue. Slippery tongue. That was always her problem. Thank goodness.

Camilla Inconsiderate gender identification must be the bane of your life.

Lucy On the slopes of linguistic slippage, I've become as nimble as a chamois.

Camilla It must drive you mad. It's insidious, insulting.

Lucy Well; I'm no longer as offended as some insist I have the right to be.

Gilly Me neither.

Hetty Anyway, I'm sorry.

Alex The point is, you're welcome here.

Camilla Why wouldn't she be?
Tim Hear, hear.
Jake Bottoms up.
Magdalena More the merriest.
Jeff (*Raises his glass.*)
Gilly Welcome! You're welcome.

Lucy Thank you.

Alex Whoever you are, and whatever, whoever you want to be, I mean, present . . .

Camilla Would you like a spade, Alex?

Alex Present! That's the bloody word.

Pause.

Jake Did you catch any of the England-Wales?

Tim I didn't, no.

Jake Thirty-six twelve, apparently.

Tim England?

Jake Wales.

Tim Ah.

Pause.

Lucy I'm grateful for the acknowledgement, Alex; and however awkward, it deserves another. I have not passed. There was a time I dreamt of doing so on a daily basis, but wishing rarely made it so. Some magical times, in a bar, or Selfridges. But never on a bus, or in the laundromat. The years I dreamed. Then an unthinking cruelty and I'd bid farewell to Carphone Warehouse, hello to Jo Malone. A hidden thought expressed with thoughtless words, and I'd move on to Hotel Chocolat. I searched for the shop floor that best supported my heels. I would stride in hope, or wade through the day's disappointments. Eventually I came to rest behind the counter of Coco de Mer, without a care.

Alex Which is where we met, he confessed.

Lucy It was indeed. I suspect amidst the seductive, selective downlighting of my little erotic emporium, Alex, I appealed to you. Which maybe in the candlelit living room of suburban sex, I might not. Maybe you made an error of judgement, but then again, maybe I did. For which, you'll understand, I may not apologise, for to do so would make my very life a mockery.

Alex Lucy; you have great sales technique and a fine taste in underwear.

Hetty Underwear?

Alex You're wearing it. I enjoyed meeting you a great deal. And yes. You passed.

Lucy I did?

Alex Like a parade.

Tim Terrific. Bravo.

Lucy Time was I would have craved that. And all sorts of things. Now all I crave is your respect.

Camilla You have it.

Magdalena If I was a man I would *be* a transvestite.

Jeff Have you checked recently?

Magdalena Me? Or You!

Camilla Such a pejorative term.

Lucy A cross-dresser is a man in woman's clothes. Do I *look* like a man in woman's clothes?

   Pause.

Camilla No, you don't.
Hetty No.
Gilly No.
Tim No, no.

Lucy I wasn't asking for a show of hands.

Jeff It depends on the lighting, presumably.

Lucy Oh, doesn't it just?

Alex Jeffrey? May I call you Jeffrey? Mind your p's and q's, mate.

Lucy I understand your confusion.

Jeff That's good, because I'm not at all sure I understand *yours*.

Lucy I'm not confused. I *was* confused, for many years. Like most kids, I tried on my mother's clothes, only to discover my inner longing could never be satisfied in Marks and Spencer's.

Alex You don't need to expalin yourself to us. This is not some suburban backwater with pampas grass in the front garden. This is Islington. My house. And an inclusive space.

Jake And that means anything goes then, does it?

Alex It's a consensual space, also. Obviously.

Tim I'm a bit confused, if truth be known.

Camilla What's happening, Tim, is some people are deliberately failing to distinguish between sexual orientation and gender identity.

Jeff Not me.

Tim They're two different things then, are they?

Camilla Yes, Tim.

Jeff Sexual orientation is determined by a number of factors, such as: are you attracted to men or women, do you like musicals, and do you put up your own shelves?

Camilla Wrong. Even in jest.

Jeff Whereas being transgender is about *identity*.

Camilla Correct. Please don't conflate the two.

Jeff *You* ever conflate the two, Luce?

Jake May I speak for the men here?

Gilly No.
Hetty No.
Alex No. Please, God.

Jake No really, I'm genuinely interested, and ignorant. How would you describe yourself?

Camilla Lucy's a woman.

Lucy That's not what he's asking.

Tim Not like *Drag Race* then?

Camilla NO.
Alex NO.

Tim No, *not*. That's what I said.

Lucy There's no need to be confused, Tim. I'm a woman, Jake.

Gilly And what am I?

Pause.

Hetty Well, you both look fabulous anyway.

Gilly And if we look fabulous, everything's fabulous.

Lucy I understand your various anxieties . . .

Jeff I'm not anxious.

Lucy Some of you boys are concerned I might come on to you. And I'm sure the ladies are equally anxious to know, should we play together, what toys we might be playing with. Which brings us to the question that is obsessing you and rendering some of you incapable of rational thought. That burning question in the forefront of all your minds.

Jake Which is?

Lucy Does she still have a cock?

Room silenced by this truth bomb.

Which is, ironically, an enquiry made of me with far greater alacrity in the big bad outside world than it has been here this evening.

Jake Okay. Now I'm anxious. Man enough to admit it. And the answer is?

Lucy Would you like my habitual reply?

Jake Sure.

Lucy That it's none of your business. Does anyone have any drugs?

Alex Sorry, no.
Hetty Not really.
Gilly We don't, no.
Jake A ciggy a day, on the doorstep . . .
Camilla Not on me, no.
Jeff You do drugs?
Magdalena Drugs! Let's have drugs!

Magdalena He never buys me drugs.

Tim I do, as a matter of fact. In my trouser pocket.

Lucy Where are your trousers?

Tim In the tumble dryer. Oh, shit.

Alex Cocaine's in the quiche, or I'd go straight for the heroin in the hummus.

Exit Tim.

Jeff Under these particular circumstances, is 'none of your business' a valid response?

Lucy Certainly. Unless you make it your business, of course.

Jake That's hardly reassuring.

Jeff But either way, may we presume you are attracted to men?

Lucy Not all of them.

Camilla This is nobody's business but your own.

Lucy It's been something of a journey, I'll admit. In my younger days I was occasionally attracted to women. Then I hit the oestrogen and things became increasingly vague. Then came the anti-androgens, which profoundly affected my libido.

Gilly What are they, exactly?

Lucy Pills. One of them makes you lunch on salad and buy handbags. The other makes you HATE *Breaking Bad*.

Gilly No, that's the oestrogen. It's such a curse.

Jake Certainly is.

Gilly Stop it.

Jeff You're saying you swing both ways?

Lucy I'm not sure. No one has pushed my swing in quite a while. It hangs vertically in the middle of the playground. I sit on it. Wild with expectation.

Alex Well, it's the swings or the roundabout, I suppose.

Enter Tim.

Tim Disco biscuit. I'd just take a half if I were you.

Lucy That'll do nicely. Thank you.

Alex Do you *have* to do drugs?

Tim Yes. Anyone else?

Jake Heaven forfend.

Lucy and Tim share a tab.

Jeff So *do* you still have a cock?

Pause.

Alex Now, that's enough.
Hetty You did *not* just say that.
Camilla That's extremely offensive.
Jake Fair question.
Gilly Seriously?
Tim Does who have a cock?
Magdalena Do *you*, my darling?

Alex You can't just ASK SOMEONE THAT.

Lucy Well, maybe not most people.

Hetty I don't care if you've got one or not. But I LOVE your eyeshadow.

Lucy Charlotte Tilbury.

Hetty I knew it. I really *do* hate you.

Jeff Well?

Camilla It's none of your business.

Jeff I was asking on behalf of the group.

Magdalena How magnanimous.

Camilla Not on my behalf, thank you.

Lucy Let's put it this way. I was invited to a sex party. I wasn't going to come, and then I did. I could tell you the reasons I was going to, but am currently clueless. But let me clarify my *desires* by way of an invite. If any of you are sufficiently curious as to my ownership or otherwise of a 'cock' . . . feel free to find out.

Jeff That's exceedingly generous of you.

Jake I think I'll pass.

Gilly Don't be so rude.

The role of **Magdalena** is now being played by
Amanda Ryan

Lucy Or you could all take a vote and I could get an Uber.

Camilla No, no.
Alex No, no, no; it's cool.

Hetty It *is* cool. Isn't it?

Jake Fine by me.

Gilly It's fine by everyone.

Jake Well, you can't speak for everyone.

Gilly Can't I? You can. It's more or less your *raison d'être*.

Jeff Strictly theoretically, I can imagine that for some people this would not be in the least *cool*.

Alex Cool is what I said, for the first time in my life, and cool is what I meant.

Camilla You are welcome here. Full stop.

Alex Hear, hear.
Hetty Absolutely.
Jake Right.
Gilly One hundred per cent.

    Pause.

Jake In any case; it's time we were off.

Alex Already? Are you going?

Jake Early start.

Gilly Do we?

Jake The kids.

Gilly . . . are with your mother.

Jake In any case.

Tim Should we head off?

Camilla No.

Gilly You can go if you want to.

Lucy I'd be happy to leave.

Gilly No. You're staying.
Alex No, no. You're staying.
Hetty You're definitely staying.

Gilly So am I.

Jake Alright. We'll stay.

Hetty So, what? Are we all going to stay in the kitchen now or what?

Jeff Good question. Alex?

Alex What?

Jeff Well, it's your kitchen. What do you think?

Alex I think we should all move through into the living room.

Camilla Bravo.

Gilly Righto.
Hetty Whoopee.
Magdalena I am a lesbian now; remember.

Gilly Me too.

Jake If you say so.

Gilly What?

Jake Whatever you say.

Camilla I feel rather more liberated, Tim. But I will need a top-up.

Hetty Cold one in the fridge!

Jeff I might smoke a cigarette.

Tim I've got the munchies, actually.

Jake Could I bum one?

Tim Have you got any Frosties or anything?

Alex Cheerios.

Tim Cheerios! Wow.

Alex Help yourself.

Tim Cheerios. Excellent.

No one has left the room.

Magdalena My husband's a bully. I ignore him. Soon he will sulks, and not realise you're ignoring him. He doesn't like homosexuals.

Lucy That's not what I am.

Magdalena Of course you are, darling. With delusions of grandness.

Camilla That is deeply ignorant.

Lucy Deeply dangerous, also.

Jake Dangerous how?

Magdalena Is not head, is heart.

Tim I know what I'd like to know. Not being contentious, but what do you think about the J. K. Rowling thing? Are you on her side or Harry Potter's?

Camilla You are twelve years old; do you know that?

Lucy You mean I am what I am unless you say I'm not?

Hetty Alex and I were discussing this.

Alex In passing.

Hetty I don't know what I think, but Alex strongly believes . . . something. Don't you?

Alex I think it's complicated.

Lucy In what way, *complicated*?

Gilly Is it? Has anyone actually read what she wrote?

Alex More wine, anyone? More beer?

Hetty You said . . .

Alex Alright. I said. What I said. If we're being honest. The nub of the issue as I see it, is . . . you can be whoever you like, but please, don't purloin the language.

Hetty Purloin.

Lucy In what way?

Alex Well . . . okay. You go to the bathroom in a restaurant.

Lucy That's a good example.

Alex It is. On the door there's a woman. Or a man.

Lucy Or a witty thematic pictogram you have to stare very hard at, and then guess.

Alex Yes.

Lucy Welcome to my world.

Hetty I use either.

Lucy Well, so do I.

Gilly Be my guest. I identify with the shortest queue.

Alex I don't want to get into the politics of it.

Lucy Thank heavens for that.

Alex But a fridge is a fridge. It's not a door.

Lucy Neither am I.

Alex Precisely. This is beer, not gin. So we call it beer. If it was gin we would call it gin. How else would we know the difference?

Lucy You could taste it.

Gilly Has anyone read what she wrote?

Alex Words are the shared parameters of our humanity.

Lucy You've not heard some of the words I've heard.

Hetty Alex. Come and do things.

Alex Sit where you like on the gender spectrum, obviously.

Lucy Thank you kindly. But I think the spectrum you're imagining is rather monochrome. The one we propose is more . . . a rainbow!

Jeff How nice for it.

Alex I'm on a high horse, I know. It's a long way down.

Gilly The thing is, you've got, what? Seventy pronouns to choose from?

Lucy What have you got against my pronouns?

Gilly What have you got against mine?

Jeff You really need hers?

Gilly Don't agree with me! I'd rather not agree with you.

Jeff Fall foul of the pronoun police . . .

Alex And apparently that's verbal discrimination.

Jeff Which is an offence.

Alex And a HATE CRIME, apparently.

Hetty Well, then; don't do it, then you haven't, and it isn't.

Lucy Thank you, Hetty. That's very Islington of you.

Tim I bloody love Islington. Couldn't afford it. And with Brighton, you know, there's the sea and that.

Camilla I don't think you've anything further to contribute, Tim.

Tim googles.

Alex Language is fluid but you cannot legislate for pronouns.

Jeff That's like shooting someone in the head for not saying sorry.

Lucy Or just minding their own business.

Jeff Freedom of speech is the prime concern here.

Alex I agree with him but I don't agree with anything he says.

Camilla Oh, freedom of speech. That old chestnut.

Hetty Oh, please; let's not.

Camilla No, I'm sorry. There are things that should NOT be said.

Jeff Which I also don't agree with, but that's another issue.

Camilla The N-word!

Jeff What?

Camilla Is that a word you'd use?

Jeff In context, of course.

Camilla The Holocaust?

Jake The what?

Jeff The Holocaust?

Camilla Happened.

Hetty Oh, not the Holocaust.

Camilla You can't just say it didn't.

Jeff I'm not arguing for the right to dissemble. Quite the opposite. This entire debate is just a left-wing ploy to gain linguistic supremacy.

Gilly Left-wing? I don't think so.

Jeff Go far enough left, where do you end up?

Jake Good point.

Gilly Don't side with him!

Jeff Political compassion's a clown mask. I ain't wearing it.

Lucy May I ask, if freedom of speech is the issue; what pronoun would you currently use when referring to me?

Jeff I would use the pronoun that reflects the persona you're choosing to project.

Lucy Well, that's nice to know.

Jeff Don't thank me; it's a party. In a more formal situation I might need to ascertain if your request was some ideological game, or a genuine concern regarding your perceived identity.

Lucy Well . . . take your best guess.

Jeff I don't want this to get personal.

Lucy Well, that's a relief.

Tim Here we go. Alphabetical order: Agender, Androgynous, Bigender, Cis . . . that's me, right?

Jake That's most of us.

Lucy Ha.

Tim Cross-dresser, Gender-nonconforming, Questioning, Variant, Queer, Male, Female . . .

Gilly Thank you. That's me. That's all I'm saying.

Alex Tim . . .

Tim Pansexual, MTF.

Jake What's that?

Alex What *is* that?

Tim Doesn't say.

Lucy Mild-mannered to Furious.

Tim Gender-bender, Gender-blender, Gender-fluid.

Hetty Eurgh.

Tim Intersex, Non-binary, Neither.

Hetty You can be that as well? You can be Neither?

Camilla In Tim's case, less than.

Tim Thank you. Other, Pangender, Transgender . . . blimey.

Alex Spoilt for choice, really.

Lucy Trust me, that's not how it feels.

Tim Trans Female, Trans Male . . .

Alex If he scrolls down again he's going in the fire-pit.

Tim Trans Person, Transsexual, Two-spirit.

Hetty Ooh.

Lucy Two-spirit.

Hetty I'll be that. What is that? Can I be that?

Camilla You can be anything you like.

Lucy No. You can be anything you *are*.

Alex Precisely!

Gilly That's all I want to be, and all of a sudden I'm a fascist.

Camilla Maybe, and this *would* simplify things, maybe you're just transphobic.

Gilly I'm not! I'm bullied and bewildered!

Jeff Look, this is not a trans-anything issue.

Lucy It's not a trans-anything issue for you because you ain't one. But we do exist.

Jeff I'm not *saying* you don't exist.

Lucy Oh! Wakes up in a cold sweat. It was all a dream.

Gilly I've been assaulted on the Tube, I've been belittled by mechanics, harassed in bars and ignored in board meetings. I've given birth twice and, guess what? I've never been asked for my pronouns.

Jake Because no one gets a word in edgewise.

Gilly Please just . . . stop it.

Jake Sorry. I was joking. That's all I was doing. I'm on your side. Seriously. If this was Wimbledon.

Camilla What?

Tim Right! If this was tennis and you could play tennis, you could probably trounce Gilly here.

Jake Definitely. With your wrong hand.

Tim I mean, so . . . do you think that would be entirely fair?

Camilla Oh, shut up, Tim. I mean could you just . . . shut the fuck up.

Jeff Let me say this . . .

Hetty I don't think you should, whatever it is.

Lucy Say it.

Jeff Make up whatever words you want. Be a Zie, Zim, Zir, be a Tey, Ter, Tem, be Terself or Emself. I don't care.

Lucy I'm impressed.

Jeff But you can't have the words that exist already. They're ours.

Gilly Woman.

Jeff Alex?

Alex Words are words.

Awkward silence.

Lucy Alex, are you happy I'm here?

Alex I'm perfectly happy you're here.

Lucy But your language excludes me; do you see?

Alex But language is language. And words . . . are how I *think*.

Lucy Yes. And now you're being asked to think something else ON BEHALF OF SOMEONE ELSE. To alter your thinking for the good of someone YOU ARE NOT. Tough one, huh?

Hetty Why don't we stop talking and take our clothes off?

Jake After you.

Magdalena We have big pile of pronouns. Let's fuck each other in it.

Jeff Identity is a thing one *negotiates*.

Lucy Bye-bye Selfridges – hello, M&S.

Jeff There are paths through the woods for a reason.

Lucy A path is just a route well-trodden. There are an infinite number of routes.

Jeff And sooner or later an infinite number of people lost in the woods.

Camilla So we should all stick to your path?

Jeff Well, that path is a thousand years old, and for good reason.

Camilla Well, I want to see the world transformed . . .

Jeff And I wish Christmas wasn't the colour of Coca-Cola. But self-identification poses a genuine threat to the stability of the nuclear family.

Camilla The nuclear family is a very dull soap opera. There are same-sex families, polyamorous families . . .

Jeff Imitations. Plaster casts of the original concept.

Jake True enough.

Gilly DON'T SIDE WITH HIM.

Jake Was I? I don't think I was.

Jeff Yes, you were. Men and women bond to conceive and raise children in a viable social unit.

Lucy And attend the occasional sex party.

Jeff Nothing wrong with a little transgression, Luce.

Hetty You should just shut up. You're horrible.

Camilla A homophobe.

Hetty With a horrible dick.

Lucy What a delightful conversation. Entirely appropriate to a nice house in Islington with articulate people. But elsewhere, in some dark, late-night street, the inarticulate echo of this conversation will get a person just like me – killed.

Gilly I've walked those streets.

Lucy Not in these heels.

Gilly I need another drink.

Alex I think we should change the subject.

Lucy So do I. Let's talk about this evening. Do you not think your championing of marriage is a little at odds with your lifestyle choice?

Jeff I drop a bomb; you throw a hand grenade.

Jake Boom. Gotcha.

Lucy And you know what you are? You're the homophobe in the room.

Jake No, I'm not.

Lucy Kinda.

Jake I'm NOT.

Jeff You have an opinion on my lifestyle. I'd like to know what you think.

Jake So would I.

Jeff We'd like to know.

Lucy You really want to know what I think?

Alex I'm not sure I do. Do we?

Hetty Yes. I do.

Camilla We all do; yes.

Lucy I think 'swingers' is a very *jolly* word.

Alex I remember jolly.

Hetty I'm jolly. Aren't I?

Lucy This isn't so much an observation as a pre-conception. You may even consider it a prejudice.

Alex Well, we wouldn't want that.

Lucy 'Swingers' is a jolly word because it's meant to be. It's what *wife swappers* call themselves.

Gilly We're not doing swapping.

Lucy You call yourselves swingers because then you don't have to use the words 'wife', or 'swapping'. But 'wife swappers' is what you are.

Gilly But we're not.

Jake Husband swappers, maybe.

Alex I haven't got a wife to swap.

Lucy It's an evocative phrase. Redolent of car keys in a Murano glass bowl on an Eames coffee table.

Alex I blame John Updike.

Camilla I blame the hippies.

Lucy Ah . . . free love.

Tim I'd have been a *great* hippy.

Camilla Long-haired, beta-male sensitives convincing a generation of wide-eyed Joni Mitchell wannabes that it was the cool thing to spread their legs.

Lucy That it was hip to hop from bed to bed. That choosing was for losers.

Camilla 'Baby.'

Lucy That was the word. Smoke this, baby.

Camilla Lift that tie-dyed chiffon, baby.

Lucy You can keep your beads on, baby.

Camilla And it worked.

Lucy And the married men were furious.

Camilla A sea of tie-dyed pussy begging for it, and there they were, stuck in *The Dick Van Dyke Show*.

Lucy So. How to get laid and stay married?

Camilla Swap the wife. Make that the price for a well-stocked cocktail cabinet, and an annual trip to Disney.

Lucy The women were complicit; bored witless. It was that or Prozac. Usually both.

Camilla They got swapped, but four decades later they got wise.

Lucy So the guys got wise and the sw- word went from -opped to -ingers. Swingers are swappers. It's your ancestry. So this is what you're doing here. You're swapping the women.

Hetty I'm not being swapped. I'm doing the swapping.

Lucy That's what you're *meant* to think.

Hetty I'm swapping him. Any takers?

Camilla You've been granted the illusion of choice, but this is not of your choosing.

Hetty Well, you speak for yourself.

Camilla I'm speaking *for* you.

Hetty Well, don't! You're here too.

Tim Ah, touché.

Camilla You can shut up and grow a pair.

Tim I've got a pair, thank you.

Camilla Where are they?

Hetty In your pocket, probably.

Alex I think either we get the Monopoly out or the party's over. Or Jenga. I've got Jenga.

Hetty gets up and goes to Lucy, and kisses her deeply and deliberately.
Tim pushes Camilla against the fridge and kisses her. She resists, then surrenders. Gilly observes this, then does much the same to Jake.

Magdalena Thank Christ in heaven and about time too.

Magdalena grabs Hetty and kisses her.

Bring your boyfriend to the living room.

Hetty kisses Alex.

90

Jake Hello, wife.

Gilly Hello, husband.

Camilla pulls Tim out of the room.
Jake throws Gilly over his shoulder and follows.

Magdalena Bring your boyfriend to the living room.

Hetty Living room.

Alex What for?

Hetty drags Alex out of the room. Magdalena follows,
pushing him.

Magdalena She's going to fuck you then I'm going to fuck
you then you're going to fuck her.

Jeff and Lucy left alone, look at one another.

Jeff Nothing personal.

Exit Jeff.
Lucy checks herself in a mirror, and freshens her lipstick.
Finds Alex's phone, finds 'The Arrival of the Queen of
Sheba' on Spotify. Downs a gin, and follows the rest.

SCENE TWO

11.30 p.m.
Jeff enters with Magdalena by the wrist.

Jeff We're leaving.

Magdalena Because why, because . . .

Jeff Find your coat. Where's your coat?

Magdalena I will have bruises.

Jeff That's not all you might have.

Magdalena You are HOMOPHOBE.

91

Jeff There is such a thing as SEXUAL HYGIENE.

Jeff calls an Uber.
Enter Alex and Hetty.

Hetty You think I'm fat.

Alex I don't think you're fat.

Hetty You think I'm stupid.

Alex I don't think that.

Jeff I apologise.

Hetty I thought the whole point . . .

Alex This isn't the moment . . .

Hetty . . . was for us to have sex!

Alex . . . for a bloody domestic.

Jeff You have my apologies.

Alex I think on balance . . .

Jeff We're leaving.

Alex I think you should leave.

Hetty Why won't you have sex with me?
Magdalena I have done nothing!

Alex You've had more than enough!
Jeff You've done more than enough!

Hetty BUT NOT WITH YOU! It's you I want sex with and
we never have sex.

Alex Oh, share it with the world, why don't you?

Enter Gilly from the garden.

Gilly Well, this was a great idea.

Hetty His idea, not mine.

Gilly Thanks for the invite.

Alex You're welcome.

Gilly We must do it again some time.

Hetty Well, you got what you came for.

Gilly And what would that be?

Alex Don't you two start.

Hetty We go to this ridiculous . . .

Alex Ridiculous?

Hetty RIDICULOUS EXTREME, this / COMPLETE CHARADE . . .

Alex Could we please just / do this later?

Hetty So that you can jump-start your PATHETIC libido . . .

Alex You've had far too much to drink!

Hetty . . . because you just don't FANCY me!

Alex So; are you two off?

Jeff Yes, we are.

Magdalena No; I'm not.

Jeff Eight minutes.

Hetty I have bent over backwards for you and you won't even TRY.

Alex You know why?

Hetty Why?

Alex Because you're so fat, obviously. Nothing to do with our dodgy compatibility or your neediness or my failure to commit.

Hetty You know what?

Alex Fuck me?

Hetty Fuck you.
Alex Fuck you too . . .

Hetty Well, chance would be a fine thing, wouldn't it?

Enter Jake from the garden.

Jake Get your coat, then.

Gilly You get it.

Jake Where are the coats?

Alex Front bedroom.

Jake And take that look off your face.

Alex I'll get them.

Gilly What look?

Exit Alex.

Jake That look that gets stuck on your face for days on end, as if I'd just shot your dog.

Gilly I was just assaulted.

Jake You were not just assaulted.

Gilly It was NON-CONSENSUAL.

Jake How could it be? I'm your husband.

Gilly Oh, so you just presumed?

Jake We're at a bloody sex party.

Hetty Are we? I hadn't noticed.

Magdalena You turn your back; boys will be boys.

Jeff I wish they would.

Gilly You were out of order!

Jake Don't blame me for having sex at a sex party!

Gilly We're supposed to be on the same page.

Jake Your page.

Gilly Our page!

Jake Whose idea WAS THIS?

Enter Tim.

Tim Alex? Where's Alex? Bit of a problem in the living room.

Enter Camilla.

Camilla You sucked her cock!

Tim Well, a bit.

Camilla YOU SUCKED her COCK!

Tim Yes, but . . . not *OFF.*

Camilla Why did you DO THAT?

Tim Well, it was . . . in my face!

Camilla Oh, so obviously . . .

Tim Seemed rude not to.

Camilla You PUT IT IN YOUR MOUTH.

Enter Alex.

Alex I don't know whose is which. I don't care much.

Enter Lucy.

Lucy Party's back in the kitchen, then?

Silence.

Gilly Lovely evening, Alex. Unforgettable.

Jake If you're going to end a sixteen-year marriage, it's nice to do it in public.

Gilly Fine by me.

Alex Look. Admittedly. These things can sometimes turn a bit wobbly.

Gilly A bit bloody wobbly?

Alex But at the end of the day, we're all good friends.

Jake Don't push your luck. And don't touch my wife!

Alex Consent sought, permission denied, no harm done. That wasn't difficult, was it?

Jake Consent to punch you in the face, please?

Lucy Denied.

Alex Thank you.

Gilly Now he asks. Maybe you should have sought consent before you put your fingers in my underwear.

Jake You like my fingers in your underwear.

Gilly NOT WHEN MY ATTENTION'S ELSEWHERE! In future keep your fingers to yourself!

Jake Well, if you must know, Ms Widdecombe, they weren't my fingers.

Gilly They weren't what?

Jake They were Tim's fingers, as it happens.

Gilly Tim's?!
Camilla Tim's?
Alex Tim's?

Tim Sorry.

Alex Bloody hell, Tim. CONSENT, for Christ's sake.

Tim I didn't not ask.

Gilly Well, you didn't ask ME.

Camilla Or me.

Jake No, he asked me. He raised his eyebrows as much as to say, and I gave him the nod.

Tim He did give me the nod.

Gilly Who are you to give him the bloody NOD?

Jake I'm your bloody husband.

Alex Start on the same page, stay on the same page. Don't just riffle through.

Jake Riffle through? She's torn out half a chapter.

Alex And you've burnt the book, mate . . .

Jake Same room sex; that's people in a room having sex, right?!

Gilly Not furtive finger sex.

Tim Was it? Sorry. I just . . .

Camilla Well next time, DON'T.

Tim I won't.

Camilla Next time, ASK.

Tim I'll ask.

Camilla And don't think ASKING makes everything okay!

Tim Doesn't it?

Alex Yes.

Camilla Not necessarily.

Alex No; if she says so.

Tim You mean *asking's* not necessarily okay, or . . .

Camilla DON'T TWIST MY WORDS.

Tim I'M TRYING TO UNTWIST THEM.

Jake He had permission.

Gilly He did not have permission.

Camilla There's a word for that.

Hetty Don't say that word.

Tim What word's that?

Hetty PLEASE don't say that word.

Alex If you say that word I will have to put you in a cab.

Camilla The word is RAPE.

Hetty No no no no no.

Alex Let's keep things in perspective.

Gilly I'm not making that sort of a fuss, but there are boundaries.

Jake Don't look at me. You're the swinger.

Gilly I'm not a fucking swinger.

Jake Well, you do a pretty good impersonation.

Camilla Your living room is a crime scene!

Alex Well, that's a bit rich.

Jake What about Alex?

Gilly What about Alex?
Jake Did *he* have your consent?

Gilly He would have. If you hadn't dragged me away. If you hadn't turned me over and offered me elsewhere!

Jake But you would have.

Gilly I might have.

Jake You fully intended to. That's why we came in the first place. Isn't it?

Hetty Is it?

Alex No. It was just one possibility in a Pandora's box of earthly delights.

Jake Dress it up like a ball pond, it's still a mosh pit.

Jeff Four minutes.

Magdalena I wish I had never met you. This is a deep-down thing.

Jeff It's mutual.

Magdalena Men ADORE me.

Jeff Not this one.

Magdalena I am rat in trap, you think. Not even rat! / I am BAIT FOR YOUR TRAP!

Jeff You meet a woman in a bar in Gdansk: AGREE THE MOTHERFUCKING PRICE. / THAT was my mistake!

Magdalena Meet my little Russian doll! You want to fuck my little / Russian whore?!

Jeff I'd re-read the pre-nup if I were you. / Before you mouth off for much longer.

Magdalena You are NOTHING inside. You are DEAD inside!

Jeff When did I last see you sober?

She grabs his wallet, pulls money from it.

Magdalena You own me? Look: your dead heart. THIS IS WHAT I THINK OF WHAT YOU THINK!

She tears the money up.

Jeff That's YOUR fucking money, honey. That's coming straight out of your allowance.

Magdalena I do credit card, you hit me?! I HATE YOU, FUCKING RICH MAN.

Pause.

Jake Forty-five minutes.

Lucy I think we should all remember that life's a lonely thing, and love's a neurosis, affection's elusive, but respect is the essential thing.

Camilla I think we can forgo any quaint philosophy from you, thank you very much.

Lucy Rude.

Alex I think what Camilla means is . . .

Camilla Oh please, yes; explain to me what I mean.

Alex I wasn't explaining to you, I was explaining to Lucy . . .

Lucy Then please don't.

Alex Obviously. No. Musn't do that.

Lucy Have I done something to offend you?

Camilla You kissed me.

Lucy Yes, I did.

Camilla A woman's kiss, I thought.

Lucy It was.

Camilla A woman's caress. Which I sought to return.

Lucy Thank you.

Camilla I glanced down to see what Tim was up to.

Tim Sorry.

Camilla And all of a sudden, I wasn't kissing a woman any more.

Lucy Yes you were.

Camilla I beg to differ.

Lucy I am a woman, with a penis.

Gilly Well, that's ridiculous.
Alex I can't get my head round that.
Camilla No. No, no no.
Jake Beam me up, Scotty.
Jeff And there it is.

Magdalena I wish.

Jeff Linguistic, sociological, biological, on every level. A complete contortion.

Lucy Why does that BOTHER you so much?

Jeff It's a distortion of reality.

Lucy Whose?

Jeff Mine!

Lucy I'd slap your face but you'd probably hit back.

Jeff I'd never hit a woman.

Lucy Well, that's encouraging. And here she is. In front of you. If you can't imagine her, it's not because you can't *see* her.

Camilla I saw a penis.

Lucy So did Tim.

Tim Yes, well, but it wasn't . . . I mean, well, it was but, well; you know what I'm trying to say. Sorry.

Lucy Tim likes my penis. I'm sure Jeff and Alex like theirs. I don't know what they've got against mine, unless they think it makes theirs somehow less . . . special.

Jeff I will not deny reality for the sake of your so-called 'identity'!

Lucy Because you're too busy denying it for the sake of your own.

Magdalena Uber is disappeared.

Jeff Goddammit!

Camilla I hate to have to say it, but this is where Jeff and I find common ground.

Lucy Could we just clarify: is your problem with my lesbian tendencies or my penis?

Camilla There is no such thing as a lesbian with a penis!

Alex I think we've all had a bit too much to drink.

Camilla My oppression is not yours to fetishise!

Lucy Well, now here's the thing. My identity is not about any of YOU. It's about ME.

Jeff Whoever *you* are.

Lucy Who*ever* I am. And you can ignore me, turn away from me, run screaming out the door, but here I am.

Jeff Just because you say you *are* one does not mean that such a thing *EXISTS*.

Lucy Well, it's standing right in front of you.

Lucy puts Jeff's hand on her breast. He pushes her violently away.

Jeff 'It's'! Correct. You finally chose the right pronoun.

Lucy Party's over, sweetie.

Jeff lunges for Lucy.

Alex No.
Hetty Alex!
Jake Whoa whoa whoa.
Gilly No, no, no, no, no . . . !
Tim Bloody hell.
Camilla No violence!

> *Alex and Jake grab Jeff.*
> *Magdalena grabs a carving knife.*

Magdalena Not ever. I tell you! Not me. Not anyone.

> *Magdalena takes a few steps, knife raised, towards Jeff.*

Alex Stay back.
Hetty (*Screams.*)
Jake Now then!
Gilly Don't! Don't!
Tim Put that down!
Camilla I said no violence!

Magdalena I cut your balls off.

Jeff Well, there we have it.

Magdalena Or you want I stab it in my heart?

Jeff Make a bold choice.

> *Magdalena turns the knife to herself, the point to her*
> *heart, and runs at the wall.*
> *Everyone screams, shouts, and scatters. Except Lucy,*
> *who grabs Magdalena around the waist just before she*
> *reaches the wall, and Tim, who grabs the knife from*
> *Magdalena as Lucy swings her through the air.*

Alex Right. That's hometime, I think. It's way past bedtime.

Jeff Your hosting skills leave a lot to be desired.

Magdalena Machiavel!

Camilla You ought to be arrested.

Jake He's lucky he's not unconscious.

Gilly To be honest, Alex, you throw a shit party.

Alex You're right. Stuff from Iceland is always a disappointment. And who serves prosecco, really? The bride's parents? I've had more ludic pleasure playing Ludo. That was banter. Anyone notice? It was an interesting affair, our first sex party. Terrific host. What a nice man. A maker of mischief, the holder of safe space, a magisterial libertarian, and a bit of a wanker really. I mean, all in all, he ought to be ashamed of himself. And you know what? He is. I am. Satisfied?

> *Silence. They each find their equilibrium.*
> *Camilla, Jeff, Jake and Gilly find their phones and tap for an Uber.*

SCENE THREE

Midnight.
> *Alex and Gilly.*
> *Jeff and Magdalena are dressed to leave.*

Jeff It was great.

Alex You're welcome.

Jeff You should maybe build a dungeon in the cellar.

Alex Might come in useful.

Jeff Sorry if I mouthed off. I like to stay rational in irrational situations, if that makes any sense.

Alex It was nice to meet you. Great to meet you.

Magdalena Take our card. This is our number. This my lips. This my pussy.

Alex Thank you.

Jeff Goodnight. Bye.

Gilly Bye.

Exit Jeff.

Magdalena It was rude of me to try and kill my husband.

Alex Don't mention it.

Magdalena It is my heart. I hate my heart. Once I was butterfly. Then I was poker chip. Now I am Holic. Everything-a-holic. You think England is warm? No. As cold as marriage. You drink, you fuck, because only other thing is Harrods. Harrods I dreamed of but is everything and empty. You go to country. You have to crawl on knees to light the Agaaaagh. And all the butterflies; frozen.

Exit Magdalena.

Gilly Hey ho.

Alex You do *know*, don't you?

Gilly Know what?

Alex It was always you.

Gilly Well, hindsight's a wonderful thing.

Alex We'd have had kids . . .

Gilly Overrated.

Alex Really?

Gilly . . . No.

Alex I honestly think . . . I might have become a different me.

Enter Camilla in her coat.

Camilla Where's Tim?

Gilly He's in the garden.

Camilla Tim! The car's here.

Tim (*off*) Righto.

Camilla What can I say? It's been a divine evening. And you're lucky I haven't called the police.

Alex Get home safe.

Exit Camilla, enter Tim.

Tim Bye, then. I usually apologise before I leave anywhere, just in case. But I think I've done alright tonight. Well, relatively speaking. Sorry.

Gilly Is that an apology?

Alex Yes.

Tim Well . . . yes.

Gilly Nice to have made your acquaintance.

Alex Great to see you.

Camilla (*off*) Tim!

Tim Night, then.

Exit Tim.

Gilly You've had a good life.

Alex If you say so.

Gilly Well, at least you made the most of it.

Alex Did I? I doubt it. Unfocused desire has quite undone me. Now I sit in graveyards.

Gilly I used to sit in playgrounds. Now I drop them at Bryanston and renew my gym membership. I'm very fit for a woman of my age.

Alex Yes you are.

He kisses her.

Gilly Nice.

Alex We should have an affair.

Gilly We can't. I'm already having one.

Alex Are you?

Gilly *Fifty Shades*, I'd imagined. Alan Bennett, BBC2, Sunday night is what I got.

Alex So why not with me?

Gilly Because you wandered off. Chose someone else, then everyone else.

Enter Jake.

Jake Are you coming or what?

Gilly Coming, of course.

Jake I should have gone to Twickenham.

Gilly You could have gone to Twickenham.

Jake Shaving my balls all afternoon.

Gilly You didn't have to shave your balls. You *decided* to shave your balls.

Jake Thirty-six twelve. Thanks for the invite. You must come over for fondue some time. She does a great fondue.

Gilly Stop it.

Jake You do. She does. I'm guessing you're not the flower guy. The guy who gives her the flowers that go in the bin. I mean, what does he think she's going to do with them? Dead flowers have that smell, you know? Seriously. Fondue. Anytime. Oh: if you do get it together, remember she's bringing up two boys. Tom's a fire-starter and Giles is probably gay but they're good boys and she's brought them up. I just pay the fees and kick a ball about with 'em, really.

Gilly Please don't.

Jake (*genuinely*) I wasn't. They're great boys. Really. Thank you.

> *He throws the car keys in Gilly's lap. Exit Jake.*
> *Gilly and Alex look at each other for a long time.*

Gilly Bye, then.

Alex Bye.

> *Exit Gilly, enter Lucy.*

Lucy Hetty's passed out. I tucked her in. Shame's a killer, Alex. Shoulders up. Spit, spot. Can I help tidy up, or should I fuck off?

Alex Oh, don't bother. I'll do it.

> *Alex doesn't move. Lucy begins to tidy.*

Lucy You'd think now, wouldn't you, that my presence at a sex party would make it WAAAAY more enjoyable. But no; the party's pooped. When I was still learning make-up, a woman came up to me in the ladies' and said, 'Your eyeshadow, how do you *do* that?' I was overjoyed. I taught her. There's much to be learned. It might look like I'm filling the dishwasher, but in fact I'm reaffirming my gender role.

Alex Sorry.

Lucy No, no. I'm flattered. You sitting there on your fat backside is a beautiful acknowledgment.

> *Alex laughs. They begin to tidy the kitchen energetically, throwing stuff into bin liners.*

Alex Why *did* you come here tonight?

Lucy I'm not sure. Death wish?

> *She stops. Sits.*

Alex What?

Lucy In one week's time I shall slide under a general anaesthetic and when I awaken . . . it'll be gone. Every last ounce of her. It will have taken me thirty-eight years to arrive in the world the way I feel I should have made my entrance. Maybe that's why I came. I should call an Uber. Ubers can be fun.

Alex Stop over if you like. It's a big enough house.

Lucy It's a very big house. It's supposed to be sunny tomorrow and if I get to Hampstead Heath early enough I can annoy people at both ponds. Says the person who has had by far the least sex tonight, or my entire life, most probably. Put the kettle on, then.

  Lights.

SCENE FOUR

Eight months later.
  Alex and Hetty. Dressed sombrely.
  Hetty is eight months pregnant.

Alex You never phone. And if I phone, you don't phone back.

Hetty I don't phone anyone. Honey, it's exhausting. I'm exhausted.

Alex I thought we were closer than that.

Hetty Were we?

Alex Well, weren't we?

Hetty I don't know what we were.

Alex Well, we were good friends.

Hetty We still are.

Alex Are we?

Hetty Aren't we?

Alex We never speak. We have no relationship.

Hetty Have a baby, then get back to me.

Alex I can imagine.

Hetty fingers an order of service.

Look, I love you, obviously.

Hetty No you don't. That wasn't who we were.

Alex Is it mine?

Hetty I don't know.

Alex Whose is it?

Hetty If I don't know, I don't know. I've narrowed it down.

Alex Well, that's something.

Hetty I've narrowed it down to six.

Alex Six? Well, that's . . .

Hetty I know.

Alex That's everyone.

Hetty Well?

Alex Well what?

Hetty I mean so. So what? It was just you or 'who cares' in my mind, I think. You weren't up for it so I did all six.

Alex Tim?

Hetty Poor Tim.

Alex But Tim.

Hetty In the garden. Bit of a quickie.

Alex You're lucky she didn't catch you.

Hetty I did clandestine in the middle of an orgy. You should be impressed. I was. Tim was impressed. Oh, poor Tim? Why Tim?

Alex Asthmatic.

Hetty Tim.

Alex The American . . .

Hetty Jeff.

Alex Was at death's door, by all accounts.

Alex fixes an order of service to the fridge with a fridge magnet.

Hetty Is there anyone who didn't get it?

Alex Lucy managed not to. It was very mild for me. But no; more or less a full house.

Hetty Poor Tim.

Alex I didn't know you'd done the room.

Hetty Having been a bit of a slut by about half-past ten, I distinctly remember thinking: I'm going to do the room. So I did. It's all a bit of a blur. There was at least one while I was otherwise engaged. I'm saying six; it might have been five. But I don't know who the last one *was*, so it's probably six.

Alex You are a liberated soul.

Hetty I owe it all to you.

Alex Oops.

Hetty . . . a-daisy.

Alex When's the blood test?

Hetty Don't want one. I've had a very long talk with my mum. If they don't sell the house, I can move back in.

Alex So how do we find out who the father is?

Hetty I don't want to.

Alex You don't what?

Hetty I've thought it through. I've done a lot of thinking. I know you think I don't, and I don't much, but I can and I have.

Alex I think you'd be better off knowing.

Hetty Oh, you think?

Alex I think so.

Hetty You think YOU'D be better off knowing. Worth a roll of the dice; one-in-six chance; zero responsibility.

Pause.

Have you spoken to Jeff? Or Magdalena?

Alex They're not playing any more.

Hetty Divorce?

Alex Herpes.

Hetty Oh, not herpes; don't say herpes.

Alex Herpes.

Hetty It was fun while it lasted, I suppose.

Pause.

You don't have to say anything. Mum's cock-a-hoop. She'd given up hope. Mum and me'll be just fine, thank you.

The door slams off.
   Lucy enters with shopping.

Lucy Lapsang, Earl Grey, Fortnum's Explorer . . . spoilt for choice. Hello.

Hetty Hello.

Lucy How was the funeral?

Hetty Horrible. It was a funeral. I was just going.

Lucy I'll put the kettle on.

Hetty No thanks. It's alright. Don't see me to the door.

Alex Why not?

Hetty Mum's in the car, and she hates you. Bye, then.

Alex When will I see you?

Hetty Don't be stupid. Bye.

Lucy Goodbye.

Alex Good luck.

Exit Hetty. The door slams off.

Lucy Earl Grey?

Alex Yorkshire.

Lucy I'll pop you in some vanilla essence.

Alex Thanks.

Lucy People in love are flooded with oxytocin. If the relationship lasts, so does the chemical. The meadow vole, high oxytocin, mates for life. The prairie vole, much lower levels, a lifetime's promiscuity.

Alex Human monogamy is a social construct.

Lucy So how *is* life on the prairie?

Alex There's a drought. How's the meadow?

Lucy I wouldn't know. I'm still in the woods. An enigma and anathema. You're the word person. To transition: dictionary definition?

Alex To change.

Lucy Or to 'go beyond'. Which is maybe a place you can get to by standing very still, just where you belong. Rich tea or custard cream?

Alex No. Thank you.

Alex sits staring. Lucy strokes the back of his head.

Lucy Don't flinch.

Alex I didn't flinch.

Lucy You flinched.

Lights.
Projection: A one-year-old baby girl. Laughing, happy, comfortable in and celebrating her unfolding world.
It lasts for a minute.
Fade to black.
The End.